Governors State University
Library Hours:
Monday thru Thursday 8:00 to 10:30
Friday 8:00 to 5:00
Saturday 8:30 to 5:00
Sunday 1:00 to 5:00 (Fall
and Winter Trimester Only)

(continued)

Beginning School

U.S. POLICIES IN INTERNATIONAL PERSPECTIVE

EDITED BY

Richard M. Clifford
Gisele M. Crawford

Teachers College, Columbia University
New York and London

Published by Teachers College Press, 1234 Amsterdam Avenue, New York, NY 10027

Copyright © 2009 by Teachers College, Columbia University

Library of Congress Cataloging-in-Publication Data

Beginning school : U.S. policies in international perspective / edited by Richard M.
    Clifford, Gisele M. Crawford.
    p. cm. – (Early childhood education series)
    Includes bibliographical references and index.
    ISBN 978-0-8077-4931-9 (pbk. : alk. paper)
    ISBN 978-0-8077-4932-6 (hardcover : alk. paper)
    1. Early childhood education–United States. 2. Early childhood education–
Government policy–United States. 3. Early childhood education–Cross-cultural
studies. I. Clifford, Richard M.
    II. Crawford, Gisele M.
    LB1139.25.B44 2009
    372.210973–dc22   2008032900

ISBN 978-0-8077-4931-9 (paper)
ISBN 978-0-8077-4932-6 (cloth)

Printed on acid-free paper
Manufactured in the United States of America

16   15   14   13   12   11   10   09   8   7   6   5   4   3   2   1

Contents

Acknowledgments

The editors gratefully acknowledge the important contributions of participants in a conference in Chapel Hill, North Carolina, where the papers that became this book were first presented: Lynette Aytch, Don Bailey, Oscar Barbarin, Donna Bryant, Virginia Buysse, Pam Cardoza, Maggie Connolly, Shelley deFossett, Jane Foust, Thelma Harms, Syndee Kraus, Kelly Maxwell, Ellen Peisner-Feinberg, Wanda Weaver, and Pam Winton (Frank Porter Graham Child Development Institute); Barbara Coatney (Chapel Hill Carrboro City School District); Carolyn Cobb (More at Four Pre-kindergarten Program); Chih-Ing Lim, William Malloy, and Sharon Palsha (University of North Carolina–Chapel Hill School of Education); Fasaha Traylor (Foundation for Child Development); and Marci Young (Center for the Childcare Workforce/ American Federation of Teachers). The success of the conference depended on essential help from interpreters Donato Fhunsu and Mayumi Sumita. We thank the Foundation for Child Development and the W. K. Kellogg Foundation for supporting the conference and the writing of this book, and Marie Ellen Larcada and her colleagues at Teachers College Press for their enthusiasm, support, and unswerving belief that we would ultimately meet our deadlines.

Introduction

In the United States we have experienced an ongoing evolution in the population served in public schools. Since the founding days of the republic, schooling has gradually expanded to serve both boys and girls, as well as children of all racial and ethnic origins. During the last half of the 20th century, public schools gradually increased the number of children who were offered kindergarten placement at age 5. During roughly this same period of time, the United States experienced a major shift in women's participation in the paid labor force and, as a result, a major increase in the need for care for children under 6 (Blau & Currie, 2004; Fullerton, 1999). Private nonprofit and for-profit entities met most of the demand. The public schools, however, also filled part of this need. Combined with new information on the extent of learning that occurs prior to age 6, highlighted by what has become known as "brain research," schools in the United States have increasingly begun serving children prior to kindergarten.

Many public schools are adding pre-kindergarten classes for 4-year-olds, sometimes including 3-year-old children as well. Examining national data sources, Clifford and colleagues (1999) estimated that nearly one million children were being served in school settings prior to kindergarten. This figure represents nearly one-fourth of the 4-year-olds in the United States. In surveys of state officials, the National Institute for Early Education Research (NIEER) found that state-funded pre-K programs served some 943,000 children in 2005–2006, two-thirds of whom were served in public schools (Barnett, Hustedt, Hawkinson, & Robin, 2006). If locally supported programs, programs specifically for children with special needs, and Head Start programs in the schools are counted, clearly many more than one million children are now in school before they start kindergarten.

The result of all these changes is that the United States has been expanding eligibility for public school both to serve a broader spectrum of the school-age population—essentially moving to true universal access for the kindergarten through grade 12 age groups—and expanding the age eligibility downward by at least 1 year. If this trend continues, in the foreseeable future, age 3 may become the typical age of entry into school in this country. The inclusion of younger children in public schools comes at "a time of unprecedented interest in identifying, deepening, and exploiting the connections between early childhood and elementary education" (Pianta, 2007, p. 5). Educators are paying increasing attention to the alignment of educational experiences for children from ages 3 through 8 in developmental as well as academic terms (Ritchie, Maxwell, & Bredekamp, in press).

Much attention has been paid to the broadening of education services to include the full population of age-eligible children (Urban & Wagoner, 2000), but less has been written about the downward extension of school. This downward extension, while driven by the societal forces described above, has not really been considered broadly as part of the move toward truly universal access to education, and little attention has been given to the philosophical, social, and educational implications of the change we are experiencing in our delivery of education to children starting at age 3. This is not the case in several other economically advantaged countries in the world, where early education is fully viewed as a part of the life-long education of the citizenry.

Early education in the United States has been greatly influenced by philosophers, theorists, and researchers from around the world. Froebel, Montessori, Piaget, and Vygotsky are all names that are well known by professionals in early education here. We have borrowed heavily from these and many others as we seek to provide high-quality early learning experiences for our children. There is much to learn from the rest of the world regarding the age of entry into school and the general historical and social forces that have led to the decisions in their countries concerning the education of young children. To help fill this void, we commissioned five international scholars to describe the situation in their countries related to early schooling, and to place them in the context of the historical and social forces that influenced the current situation.

We chose countries based on several criteria. We restricted our selection to countries that are relatively comparable to the United States in terms of economic development. We then further targeted countries that had recently examined or were in the process of examining the linkages between settings serving children from 3 to 8 years old. Finally, from a pragmatic viewpoint, we selected countries where we were able to identify scholars with competence in the area of interest. We did not provide them with a clearly defined set of points that we wanted covered in their chapters, but chose to let them identify the critical issues and decisions from within their own countries' perspectives. Thus each chapter intentionally covers somewhat different ground.

We are delighted that we were able to identify five eminently capable individuals to prepare chapters and to come to the United States to discuss the forces that have shaped decisions in their countries. Dr. Hans-Guenther Rossbach of Bamberg University in Germany describes the very long tradition of serving young children in Germany, the impact of the fall of the Berlin Wall, and other influences on early education in his country. In contrast, Dr. Reiko Uzuhashi of Kobe Women's University in Japan describes the impact of a changing economic situation and major changes in the age distribution of the population in Japan on thinking about early care and education. Dr. Michael Gaffney of the University of Otago highlights the issues of culture in the development of early education in New Zealand, and describes efforts to preserve a diverse array of options for families while centralizing aspects of oversight and funding. Dr. Véronique Francis of the Université Paris X–Nanterre traces the history and identity of French primary schools, and describes strategies for preserving the philosophy and traditions of the *école maternelle* (for children ages 2 to 6) while creating stronger linkages with elementary schools and smoother transitions for children. Dr. Inge Johansson of Stockholm University describes Sweden's incorporation of all of education, from birth through adulthood, under one Ministry of Education, preserving age 7 as the start of compulsory schooling but striving for greater linkages between preschool and school to achieve a seamless educational experience.

In addition, we have prepared chapters documenting briefly the history of early education and care in the United States; describing the forces in our country that are compelling us to examine when, where, and how children begin school; and comparing how the six countries have approached similar challenges, as well as identifying some of the unique features of each. We write this book with the hope that we can learn from the long histories and traditions of other countries as we transform the way we educate and care for young children.

REFERENCES

Barnett, W. S., Hustedt, J. T., Hawkinson, L. E., & Robin, K. B. (2006). *The state of preschool: 2006 state preschool yearbook*. New Brunswick, NJ: National Institute for Early Education Research.

Blau, D., & Currie, J. (2004). *Preschool, day care, and afterschool care: Who's minding the kids* [Working paper number 10670]. Cambridge, MA: National Bureau of Economic Research. Retrieved September 28, 2005, from http://www.nber.org/papers/w10670

Clifford, R., Early, D. M., & Hills, T. (1999). Almost a million children in school before kindergarten. *Young Children, 54*(5), 48–51.

Fullerton, H. N. (1999, December). Labor force participation: 75 years of change, 1950–1998 and 1998–2025. *Monthly Labor Review*, pp. 3–12. Retrieved June 19, 2007, from http://www.bls.gov/opub/mlr/1999/12/art1full.pdf

Pianta, R. C. (2007). Early education in transition. In R. C. Pianta, M. J. Cox, & K. L. Snow (Eds.), *School readiness and the transition to kindergarten in the era of accountability* (pp. 3–10). Baltimore: Paul H. Brookes.

Ritchie, S., Maxwell, K. L., & Bredekamp, S. (in press). Rethinking early schooling: Using developmental science to transform children's early school experiences. In O. Barbarin & B. Wasik (Eds.), *Handbook of developmental science and early schooling: Translating basic research into practice*. New York: Guilford.

Urban, W. J., & Wagoner, J. L. (2000). *American education: A history, second edition*. Boston: McGraw-Hill.

CHAPTER 1

Early Education in the United States

Converging Systems, Diverse Perspectives

GISELE M. CRAWFORD
RICHARD M. CLIFFORD
DIANE M. EARLY
STEPHANIE S. RESZKA

> They [Americans] have all a lively faith in the perfectibility of man [*sic*], they judge that the diffusion of knowledge must necessarily be advantageous, and the consequences of ignorance fatal; they all consider society as a body in a state of improvement, humanity as a changing scene, in which nothing is, or ought to be, permanent; and they admit that what appears to them today to be good, may be superseded by something better tomorrow.
>
> —Alexis de Tocqueville, 1945, pp. 409–410

The history of education in the United States is characterized by movements to expand access to a high-quality education to more children (Cuban, 1990). European colonists in the 17th and 18th centuries initiated a wide variety of independent efforts to educate children and establish schools. In the 19th century, widespread efforts were under way to firmly establish public schooling as an institution and to increase access to school for the lower classes, although most schools remained racially segregated. In the middle of the 20th century, the inherent inequities in the "separate but equal" doctrine of schooling for Black children were recognized by courts, which forced the desegregation of schools. In the latter part of the century, activism on behalf of children with disabilities achieved gains in the provision of appropriate and inclusive services. The need to provide equitable education opportunities to diverse populations remains an issue to this day. See Chapter 2 for a historical overview of early education in the United States and a review of the current policy landscape.

Recently, the drive to promote the success of all children in the United States has focused more and more on educational experiences starting at birth. Research demonstrating the power of high-quality early education experiences to bridge the gap in achievement between students of different racial and socio-economic backgrounds has generated attention from state- and national-level policymakers and resulted in increased government funding and oversight of early childhood programs. In Chapter 2 we document this major shift toward increasing public involvement in education for children under 5, at both the federal and state level. This trend has implications not only in terms of funding and governance, but also in terms of which specific institutions and professionals deliver these services and, ultimately, the experiences of children and families.

While increased public investment may be benefiting families and society through wider access to higher-quality early education programs, it has created a period of transition for the early childhood community. As in many countries, services for preschool-aged children in the United States are provided by an array of public and private providers arising from different traditions and supported by a mix of funding streams, including parent fees (Clifford, 1995) (see Chapter 2). Most parents must pay for their child's preschool or child care; the cost of full-day care can be as much as $1,000 per month. While there have been many disadvantages to this "non-system" in terms of inequitable access to affordable and high-quality services, historically this disorganization has permitted the existence of an early childhood community with a culture rooted more in ideas about human development and family support than in rating the abilities of individuals, and focused more on children's immediate well-being than on promoting future achievement. As the worlds of early childhood and primary school converge, the challenge will be to preserve the best practices and values of each. To do this, we, as a society, must determine what we want schools for young children to do for them and for society as a whole, and how best to deliver, regulate, and finance those services.

ALIGNMENT OF CHILDREN'S EDUCATION FROM AGE 3 TO GRADE 3

Approaches to Alignment

Most children in the United States are spending time in a classroom setting by age 3, in settings that range from private for-profit child care to public school, and that receive various public and private funds and varying degrees of oversight (see Chapter 2; Overturf Johnson, 2005). "At this time, the differences between elementary education and early childhood education are far greater than the similarities. For the most part, the systems have different funding streams, disparate pay scales, incongruent education and training, and unrelated national support" (Ritchie, Maxwell, & Clifford, 2007, p. 87). A variety of initiatives seek to bridge these systems, with the goal of creating smoother transitions for children and families. This adjustment could be a force for true reform in the public education system in the United States.

P–3 Education. School systems in the United States adopt various configurations of grades in their schools, based on the population served, the capacities of existing school buildings within the district, and theories about children's development and when best to present them with major transitions. A common configuration for elementary schools is kindergarten (which typically begins at age 5) through 5th grade (which typically begins at age 10). Many public schools are adding pre-kindergarten classes for 4-year-olds, sometimes including 3-year-old children as well.

Schools have a long way to go to adjust to the substantially different needs of these younger children. As schools have added younger children, there has been growing national interest in an organizational arrangement that groups pre-kindergarten classes in the same schools as classes for children up to age 8. This arrangement is known as a P–3 (pre-kindergarten through third grade) school. This arrangement is designed to ensure that the school system integrates these younger children fully into the school, that the facilities, routines, and educational approaches are appropriate for the needs of the young children, and that the program is integrated through a common set of standards and curricula. The shift to such an arrangement is slow, but appears to be gaining momentum (Bogard & Takanishi, 2005).

Alignment Across Systems. Most 3- and 4-year-olds are still served in non-public school settings. Various initiatives exist at the national level to forge improved connections between early care and education providers and the public schools their young students will attend. The National Education Goals Panel, a bipartisan body of federal and state officials and national leaders in education, identified ten keys to *Ready Schools*: "concrete policies and strategies that schools can introduce or expand, in order to create learning climates for young children from preschool through Grade 3" (Shore, 1998, p. 5). These strategies promote continuity for children and families between their early care and education settings and the schools those children will attend, and challenge schools to alter programs and practices that do not benefit children. Private foundations such as the W. K. Kellogg Foundation have invested heavily in community efforts to create these improved connections and in efforts by national organizations to provide technical assistance to schools and communities in implementing these strategies and evaluating their success (Hohmann, 2004; Ritchie et al., 2007). At the state level, there is a growing recognition that "school readiness" refers not only to the condition of children when they enter school, but also the capacity of schools to educate all children, whatever each child's condition may be (Maxwell, Bryant, Ridley, & Keyes-Elstein, 2001). For example, in 2007 the North Carolina State Board of Education adopted a definition and pathways for Ready Schools, including ongoing communication between the early care and education community and the schools, and alignment of standards and curricula for children from age 3 to grade 3. The Board recommends that elementary schools incorporate a Ready Schools plan into their state-mandated School Improvement Plan, and that representatives from community early care and education providers be included on that planning team (North Carolina Ready Schools Initiative, n.d.).

Implications of Alignment

Pedagogy. The establishment of free, compulsory public schooling in the United States was driven by economic, social, and political goals. The demand for educated workers with the skills and the disposition to be productive is an obvious impetus. Provision of free and universal education is aligned with cultural ideals regarding individual opportunity and social mobility. Early proponents of education also promoted the powerful political arguments that common educational experiences would promote unity in a diverse society, and that an educated citizenry was essential to the functioning of a democratic republic. Horace Mann exemplified the ideological and political faith of this era, placing public education at the center of a secular paradise (Tyack & Cuban, 1995). Public school pedagogy has varied considerably in response to these goals, across time and from school to school. Teacher-centered instruction, characterized by lecture- and textbook-based learning, and student-centered instruction, characterized by student discovery and exploration, have both had strong proponents since the 19th century. Dewey promoted respect for childhood and a child-centered approach to learning: "The problem is to unify, to organize, education to bring all its various factors together, through putting it as a whole into organic union with every day life" (Lascarides & Hinitz, 2000, p. 220). Political and economic crises have tended to refocus the public and political leaders on children's mastery of content and skills, their "competitiveness." Larry Cuban describes the debate over classroom pedagogy as a clash of "deeply held values about how teachers should teach, the role of content in classrooms, and how children should learn" (1990, p. 3). Current interest in closing gaps in achievement between different racial and socioeconomic groups has ushered in a new era of accountability and to a great degree revived the pedagogy debate (Brooks-Gunn, Klebanov, & Duncan, 1996; Lee & Burkam, 2002; Smith, Brooks-Gunn, & Klebanov, 1997).

The convergence of the early childhood and public school communities also adds fuel to this debate. Early childhood pedagogy in the United States has been influenced by many of the same influential scholars whose work has shaped early care and education around the globe, such as Froebel, Pestalozzi, and Montessori, but also bears the strong imprint of U.S. ideals and values. The social reformers of the 19th century influenced not only the supply but also the nature of early childhood services. The Progressive-era reformers promoted the provision of early education to lower-income and immigrant children as social responsibility, and also as a means of directing social evolution (Tyack & Cuban, 1995). Early education was largely associated with poverty until the kindergarten movement introduced a new point of view. "The identification of the kindergarten as a voluntary supplement to upper- and middle-class child rearing rather than a remedial intrusion into lower-class family life had much to do with its acceptance in this country" (Beatty, 1995, p. 52).

The pedagogy and instructional materials of Froebel provided a credible philosophical alternative to academic instruction for young children. Since the 19th century, early childhood educators have promoted the adoption of the same child-centered principles and methods in primary schools as were originally employed only in kindergartens and nursery schools. As free kindergartens became incorporated into public schools, "some school reformers hoped that the kindergarten, with its emphasis on the development of children, would influence the rigid curriculum and instruction prevailing in the elementary schools of the late nineteenth century" (Lascarides & Hinitz, 2000, p. 252).

Today, many educators fear that the reverse trend is occurring, that didactic instruction and a focus on content mastery are dominating in kindergarten and reaching into pre-kindergarten and other early childhood settings. Research indicates that the developmental appropriateness of instruction and children's environments decreases from kindergarten to 3rd grade (Maxwell, McWilliam, Hemmeter, Ault, & Schuster, 2001). As a response to this curricular push-down, there is a growing movement to promote the same learning principles valued by early childhood educators—children actively constructing knowledge through hands-on activities, participation in decision-making, and active engagement with peers and teachers—in the primary grades (Palsha et al., 2007).

Teacher Preparation and Credentials. Some teacher preparation programs in the United States are beginning to focus on the developmental continuum experienced by children through age 8 and a recognition that teachers of young children should be prepared to respond to children in developmentally appropriate ways while helping them meet challenging learning goals. Teachers in the United States are licensed by their state to teach specific ages or subjects, and there is growing interest among educators in offering licensures that combine pre-kindergarten with early elementary grades. Pennsylvania, Virginia, Washington, and Wisconsin offer a pre-K to grade 3 license; Arkansas offers a pre-K through grade 4 license (National Institute for Early Education Research, 2008).

Teachers who work in child care centers and most other settings for children prior to kindergarten have typically not been required to have a 4-year or even a 2-year degree, but in recent years the expectations for these teachers' qualifications have risen dramatically (see Chapter 2). There continues to be some degree of controversy surrounding higher education requirements for early childhood teachers. Teachers who have worked with young children for many years may not possess the resources or the inclination to pursue a formal degree, and while state and local initiatives do exist that support professional development for early childhood teachers, a vastly greater investment would be required to raise the education level of this workforce nationwide. Proponents of this trend argue that children stand to benefit and that ultimately early childhood professionals will benefit through higher pay and status. Critics worry that raising minimum education requirements will exclude many dedicated teachers and, in particular, decrease the diversity of the early childhood workforce. While some research on child care has shown that a higher level of teacher education is linked to better classroom quality when other factors are not controlled (Tout, Zaslow, & Berry, 2005), more recent work has not presented as clear a picture of the role of teacher education, "indicating that policies focused solely on increasing teachers' education will not suffice for improving classroom quality or maximizing children's academic gains" (Early et al., 2007, p. 558).

Current Issues and Public Discourse on Early Education

Issues surrounding the education of young children intersect with other highly charged social and educational issues confronting the United States, such as immigration, accountability, and the roles of individual choice and the private sector in the delivery of public services.

English Language Learners. Immigration is bringing increasing diversity to schools throughout the United States. With immigration comes the need to appropriately serve multicultural and multilingual school populations. Twenty percent of children from birth to age 17 have at least one foreign-born parent, and the proportion of children in immigrant families is over 5% in all but 11 states. At least 25% of children in immigrant families are considered to have limited English proficiency (Hernandez, Denton, & Macartney, 2007). English language learners, particularly from low-income families, are at particular risk for school performance problems, so access to high-quality and appropriate educational experiences is critical for this large and growing segment of the student population (Espinosa, Castro, Crawford, & Gillanders, 2007). The evidence base is accumulating, but more research is needed to allow educators to understand how best to promote English proficiency, home language development, adjustment to school, and academic success for diverse children across an array of contexts (Espinosa, 2007). Educators and families must pursue these goals in the context of an ever-growing English-only movement in the United States. Twenty-nine states have now adopted English as their official language (Winton, Buysse, & Zimmerman, 2007). These laws often prohibit or limit the use of children's home languages in public school and pre-kindergarten. Some advocates argue that this is a reason to preserve the diverse array of private early childhood settings, each existing within particular cultural contexts, rather than move to "a one-best system of preschooling, largely attached to the public schools" (Fuller, 2007, p. xii).

Accountability. Schools and early education programs are contending with strong pressure for accountability, from all levels of government and from the general public. There is an increasing emphasis on academic achievement in primary grades, accompanied by, at times, controversial shifts in how achievement is measured. "Standardized achievement tests are the most common measure used to assess school performance across all 50 states and the chief indicator of progress of state legislation and the No Child Left Behind Act. The public supports more extensive test use, wider reporting of results, and accountability for progress" (Walberg, 2007, p. 9). The federal government is exerting financial pressure on schools to bring up student test scores in math and reading, and in particular to close the gap in achievement between students of different racial and socioeconomic backgrounds (No Child Left Behind Act, 2001).

Accountability is reaching into classrooms for 3- to 5-year-olds in terms of school readiness, and is driving the increased public funding, delivery, and oversight of these programs. Kagan and Kauerz (2007) point to the current "research-driven focus on critical measurements of quality that have traditionally been associated with K–12 education" (p. 12), and efforts on the part of states to "coordinate and align child care, Head Start, prekindergarten, and other programs and policies that have been traditionally incongruent and categorical" (p. 17). A number of high-profile studies have shown that attendance in a child care or preschool program that is deemed developmentally appropriate according to traditional early childhood pedagogy predicts better outcomes for children in the early years of elementary school and, in some cases, into adulthood, especially for children at risk for school difficulties (Campbell, Ramey, Pungello, Sparling, & Miller-Johnson, 2002; NICHD Early Child Care Research Network, 2005; Peisner-Feinberg et al., 2001; Schweinhart & Weikart, 2002). Ironically, these studies, which seem to affirm the developmental philosophy and approaches of early childhood, have brought early childhood programs to the forefront of national and state political agendas, which in turn may be contributing to an increased focus on assessing the cognitive skills of younger and younger children, in order to help them meet "grade-level" academic expectations as young as kindergarten (Fuller, 2007).

Appropriate Assessment. Appropriately defining success for children, educators, and programs and identifying appropriate assessment measures and strategies are central to both increased accountability and serving the needs of diverse populations. The National Association for the Education of Young Children (NAEYC) and the National Association of Early Childhood Specialists in State Departments of Education (NAECS-SDE) produced a joint position paper on assessment for children from birth to age 8 (2003). In a national climate of increasing reliance on standardized test scores, their recommendation is that if we wish "to assess young children's strengths, progress, and needs, [we must] use assessment methods that are developmentally appropriate, culturally and linguistically responsive, tied to children's daily activities, supported by professional development, inclusive of families, and connected to specific, beneficial purposes" (NAEYC & NAECS-SDE, 2003, p. 2). They urge the use of multiple sources of evidence gathered over time when assessing children's progress or program effectiveness and conclude that use of individually administered norm-referenced tests with children should be limited to situations in which such measures are potentially beneficial to the child, such as identifying potential disabilities. Moreover, they contend that "calls for better results and greater accountability from programs for children in preschool, kindergarten and the primary grades have not been backed up by essential supports for teacher recruitment and compensation, professional preparation and ongoing professional development, and other ingredients of quality early education" (NAEYC & NAECS-SDE, 2003, pp. 4–5).

School Choice. While the notion of extending public school downward may be "a new front in the culture wars" (Fuller, 2007, p. xii), publicly funded prekindergarten may prove to be a test case for the school choice movement. The vast majority of children in the United States age 5 to 18 attend public school (see Chapter 2), and typically children are assigned to a specific school by the administration of the school district where they live. In some cases, children are assigned to the school that is closest to their home. In other cases, districts may try to balance the racial or economic distribution in their schools through student assignment. The United States has seen a growing movement to allow parents a greater degree of choice in where their children can attend publicly funded school. "Strong majorities of parents favor programs that enable parents to choose the schools, public or private, that their children attend, with public funding following the student" (Walberg, 2007, p. 8). Advocates for increased school choice point out that middle- and upper-class families already possess significant power to choose their children's public schools, by choosing where to live (Goodman & Moore, 2001). The ability to choose private school or to influence public school placement—"and the options from which to choose—are strongly shaped by the wealth, ethnicity, and social status of parents and their neighborhoods" (Fuller, Elmore, & Orfield, 1996, p. 187). Advocates of school choice see the consolidation of school districts[1] over the past century as having eroded parental influence over public schooling (Walberg, 2007). They point to research that shows strong parent support for greater choice (Elam, Rose, & Gallup, 1991) and studies that indicate academic gains for students participating in such programs (Peterson, Greene, Howell, & McCready, 1998).

School choice can take a number of different forms. Some school districts offer parents the opportunity to apply for admission to or enter a lottery for magnet schools or charter schools. According to the No Child Left Behind Act, when schools do not meet certain benchmarks for performance, parents of children enrolled in those schools can elect to enroll their children elsewhere. In a few communities, parents whose children meet certain risk criteria can apply publicly or privately funded vouchers or scholarships to pay tuition at private schools. "During the 2004–2005 school year, public voucher programs operated in six states and the District of Columbia and enrolled approximately 36,000 students in nearly 1,000 schools or tutoring programs. . . . Private voucher programs enrolled approximately 50,000 students in 79 programs in 2001" (Walberg, 2007, p. 36).

Education and care options for children under age 5 continue to permit a high degree of choice, and while they have traditionally been funded in large part by parent fees, state-funded pre-kindergarten programs often combine a degree of parental choice with public funding. Florida's pre-kindergarten program is like a voucher program, where public funds attach to the child and follow him to a public or private setting of the parents' choosing (Walberg, 2007). There is the potential for this type of pre-K program to influence the extension of parent choice upward into elementary schools. On the other hand, as pre-K and elementary programs become increasingly integrated, such parent-choice pre-K programs may need to be integrated into the K–12 system of school assignment.

WHAT CAN WE LEARN BY LOOKING OUTWARD?

As de Tocqueville observed, we in the United States do tend to have a progressive view of society. We believe we can create institutions or modify existing ones to achieve specific social, economic, or cultural goals. In practice, such efforts are likely to bring about a collision of opposing ideals, competing interests, and incompatible bureaucratic requirements. The current movement toward greater coordination between the early childhood sectors and public schooling is rife with many such collisions. What should be the respective roles of federal, state, and local governments, of education versus social service agencies, and of the private sector? Who should operate programs for younger students, and how should these programs be financed and governed? What are the best approaches to coordinating and aligning curriculum and instructional practices for children ages 3 to 8, and across states and communities? What are our goals for children of these ages, and how can these goals best be met for a diverse population of students? Chapters 3 through 8 allow us to see how five other nations have addressed similar questions, and how their experiences might illuminate the situation in the United States.

NOTE

1. "Since around 1925 . . . consolidation has collapsed roughly 115,000 separate school districts into about 15,000, and average school size has risen by a factor of five" (Walberg, 2007, p. 15).

REFERENCES

Barnett, W. S., Hustedt, J. T., Hawkinson, L. E., & Robin, K. B. (2006). *The state of pre-school: 2006 state preschool yearbook*. New Brunswick, NJ: National Institute for Early Education Research.

Beatty, B. (1995). *Preschool education in America: The culture of young children from the colonial era to the present*. New Haven, CT: Yale University Press.

Bogard, K., & Takanishi, R. (2005). PK–3: An aligned and coordinated approach to education for children 3 to 8 years old. *Social Policy Report, 19*(3). Society for Research in Child Development.

Brooks-Gunn, J., Klebanov, P. K., & Duncan, G. J. (1996). Ethnic differences in children's intelligence test scores: Role of economic deprivation, home environment, and maternal characteristics. *Child Development, 67,* 396–408.

Campbell, F. A., Ramey, C. T., Pungello, E. P., Sparling, J., & Miller-Johnson, S. (2002). Early childhood education: Young adult outcomes from the Abecedarian Project. *Applied Developmental Science, 6,* 42–57.

Clifford, R. M. (1995). Pßrhuzamossßgok: Napközbeni kisgyermekellßtßs az Amerikai Egyesült Államokban [Parallel play: Early childhood services in the United States of America]. In D. Katalin (Ed.), *Napjaink szociálpolitikai és társadalmi igényei a kisgyermekek napközbeni ellátásában* [Public policy, public need, and varieties of non-parental child care] (pp. 62–75). Budapest, Hungary: Bölcsódék Országos Módszertani Intezete.

Clifford, R., Early, D. M., & Hills, T. (1999). Almost a million children in school before kindergarten. *Young Children, 54*(5), 48–51.

Cuban, L. (1990). Reforming again, again and again. *Educational Researcher, 19*(1), 3–13.

de Tocqueville, A. (1945). *Democracy in America* (vol. 1). New York: Random House.

Early, D. M., Maxwell, K. L., Burchinal, M., Alva, S., Bender, R. H., Bryant, D., et al. (2007). Teachers' education, classroom quality, and young children's academic skills: Results from seven studies of preschool programs. *Child Development, 78*(2), 558–580.

Elam, S., Rose, L., & Gallup, A. (1991). The 23rd annual Gallup Poll of the public's attitudes toward the public schools. *Phi Delta Kappan, 73*, 41–56.

Espinosa, L. (2007). English language learners as they enter school. In R. C. Pianta, M. J. Cox, & K. L. Snow (Eds.), *School readiness & the transition to kindergarten in the era of accountability* (pp. 175–195). Baltimore: Brookes.

Espinosa, L., Castro, D., Crawford, G., & Gillanders, C. (2007). Early school success for English language learners: A review of evidence-based instructional practices for pre-K to grade 3. In V. Buysse & L. Aytch (Eds.), *Early school success: Equity and access for diverse learners. Executive summary* (pp. 10–13). Chapel Hill: The University of North Carolina, FPG Child Development Institute.

Fuller, B. (2007). *Standardized childhood: The political and cultural struggle over early education.* Stanford, CA: Stanford University Press.

Fuller, B., Elmore, R. F., & Orfield, G. (1996). Policy-making in the dark: Illuminating the school choice debate. In B. Fuller & R. F. Elmore (Eds.), *Who chooses? Who loses? Culture, institutions, and unequal effects of school choice* (pp. 1–24). New York: Teachers College Press.

Goodman, J. C., & Moore, M. (2001, April 27). *School choice v. school choice.* National Center for Policy Analysis Policy Backgrounder no. 155. Retrieved February 12, 2008, from http://www.ncpa.org/pub/bg/bg155/

Hernandez, D. J., Denton, N. A., & Macartney, S. E. (2007). Children in immigrant families: The US and 50 states: National origins, language and early education. *2007 Research Brief Series.* Washington, DC and Albany, NY: Child Trends and the Center for Social and Demographic Analysis.

Hohmann, C. (2004). Reentering the elementary fray: Helping schools get ready for all children. *High/Scope ReSource, 23*(2), 13–20. Retrieved February 12, 2008, from http://secure.highscope.org/Content.asp?ContentId=138

Kagan, S. L., & Kauerz, K. (2007). Reaching for the whole: Integration and alignment in early education policy. In R. C. Pianta, M. J. Cox, & K. L. Snow (Eds.), *School readiness & the transition to kindergarten in the era of accountability* (pp. 11–30). Baltimore: Brookes.

Lascarides, V. C., & Hinitz, B. (2000). *History of early childhood education.* New York: Falmer.

Lee, V. E., & Burkam, D. T. (2002). *Inequality at the starting gate: Social background differences in achievement as children begin school.* Washington, DC: Economic Policy Institute.

Maxwell, K. L., Bryant, D. M., Ridley, S. M., & Keyes-Elstein, L. (2001). *North Carolina's kindergartners and schools: Executive summary.* Chapel Hill: University of North Carolina, FPG Child Development Institute.

Maxwell, K. L., McWilliam, R. A., Hemmeter, M. L., Ault, M. J., & Schuster, J. (2001). Predictors of developmentally appropriate practices in kindergarten through third grade. *Early Childhood Research Quarterly, 16*, 431–452.

National Association for the Education of Young Children & National Association of Early Childhood Specialists in State Departments of Education (NAEYC & NAECS-SDE). (2003). *Early childhood curriculum, assessment, and program evaluation: Building an effective, accountable system in programs for children birth through age 8.* Washington, DC: Author.

National Institute for Early Education Research. (2008). *2007 state preschool yearbook interactive database: Teacher specialized training.* Retrieved March 25, 2008, from http://nieer.org/yearbook/compare/pcompare.php?CompareID=111

NICHD Early Child Care Research Network. (2005). Early child care and children's development in the primary grades: Follow-up results from the NICHD Study of Early Child Care. *American Educational Research Journal, 42*, 537–570.

No Child Left Behind Act of 2001, PL 107-110, 20 USC 6301. Retrieved July 18, 2007, from http://www.ed.gov/policy/elsec/leg/esea02/107-110.pdf

North Carolina Ready Schools Initiative. (n.d.). Retrieved March 18, 2008, from http://www.ncreadyschools.org/index.html

Overturf Johnson, J. (2005). *Who's minding the kids? Child care arrangements: Winter 2002.* Current Population Reports, P70-101. Washington, DC: U.S. Census Bureau.

Palsha, S., Ritchie, S., Sparling, J., Maxwell, K., Crawford, G., & Lim, C.-I. (2007). *A FirstSchool lens on instructional practices and curriculum: Changing schools to benefit education professionals, young children, and their families.* Unpublished manuscript, University of North Carolina at Chapel Hill.

Peisner-Feinberg, E. S., Burchinal, M. R., Clifford, R. M., Culkin, M. L., Howes, C., Kagan, S. L., & Yazejian, N. (2001). The relation of preschool child-care quality to children's cognitive and social developmental trajectories through second grade. *Child Development, 72*, 1534–1553.

Peterson, P. E., Greene, J. P., Howell, W. G., & McCready, W. (1998). *Initial findings from an evaluation of school choice programs in Washington DC and Dayton, Ohio.* Harvard University Program on Education Policy and Governance Working Paper.

Ritchie, S., Maxwell, K., & Clifford, R. M. (2007). FirstSchool: A new vision for education. In R. C. Pianta, M. J. Cox., & K. L. Snow (Eds.), *School readiness & the transition to kindergarten in the era of accountability* (pp. 85–96). Baltimore: Brookes.

Schweinhart, L. J., & Weikart, D. P. (2002). The Perry Preschool Project: Significant benefits. *Journal of At-Risk Issues, 8*(1), 5–8.

Shore, R. (1998). *Ready schools.* Washington, DC: National Education Goals Panel. Retrieved February 12, 2008, from http://govinfo.library.unt.edu/negp/Reports/readysch.pdf

Smith, J. R., Brooks-Gunn, J., & Klebanov, P. K. (1997). The consequences of living in poverty for young children's cognitive and verbal ability and early school achievement. In G. J. Duncan & J. Brooks-Gunn (Eds.), *Consequences of growing up poor* (pp. 132–189). New York: Russell Sage.

Tout, K., Zaslow, M., & Berry, D. (2005). Quality and qualifications: Links between professional development and quality in early care and education settings. In M. Zaslow & I. Martinez-Beck (Eds.), *Critical issues in early childhood professional development* (pp. 77–110). Baltimore: Brookes.

Tyack, D., & Cuban, L. (1995). *Tinkering toward Utopia: A century of public school reform.* Cambridge, MA: Harvard University Press.

Walberg, H. J. (2007). *School choice: The findings.* Washington, DC: The Cato Institute.

Winton, P., Buysse, V., & Zimmerman, T. (Eds.). (2007). Does English-only fuel achievement gap? *Early Developments, 11*(2), 18–20.

CHAPTER 2

Education for Children 3 to 8 Years Old in the United States

GISELE M. CRAWFORD
RICHARD M. CLIFFORD
DIANE M. EARLY
STEPHANIE S. RESZKA

The history of early education in the United States began with efforts to generate and institutionalize community support for education, which meant bringing education from the private sphere to the public sphere of government regulation and funding. European colonies (which then became states and territories) experienced separate evolutions from privately supported and narrowly available schooling to publicly supported and widely available (and then compulsory) education. Even when education became widely available for poor children, inequities remained in the system—in the disparity of the quality of services for rich and poor, for White children and children of color, for boys and girls, and for children with special needs. Efforts to address these inequities have been a driving force in the expansion of publicly supported services to younger and younger children.

HISTORY: EXPANDING ACCESS TO EDUCATION

Efforts Toward Public Support

In the European colonies that would become the first states of the United States of America, parents' interest in educating their children led to the propagation of dame schools and other institutions supported by parents and communities.

> We do know that . . . teachers taught part time and full time, by day and by evening, in their homes, in other people's homes, in rented rooms, in churches and meeting-houses, in abandoned buildings, and in buildings erected especially for their use; that they were self-employed and employed by others (acting as individuals or through self-constituted, self-perpetuating, or elected boards); and that they were paid with

funds obtained from employers, patrons, subscriptions, lotteries, endowments, tuition rates, and taxes. (Cremin, 1970, pp. 499–500)

In 1647 a law was passed in Massachusetts stipulating that every town of 50 families "shall appoint one within their town to teach all children . . . to write and read, whose wages shall be paid by the parents of such children . . . or by the inhabitants in general" (Cremin, 1970, p. 181). These schools were an early government effort to encourage communities to provide widespread access to public education. Though not supported with public funds, land might be set apart to support the school (Lascarides & Hinitz, 2000). In the Southern colonies very few poor children attended school. Some poor children had the chance to attend a church charity school or be apprenticed to a trade (Lascarides & Hinitz, 2000). Many of the colonial children who were educated attended schools run by ministers or under the auspices of the Society for the Propagation of the Gospel in Foreign Parts, a British organization (Urban & Wagoner, 2000).

Some tax-supported schools were available to a small number of colonial children, but most early efforts to promote free, publicly funded education took a long time to come to fruition. From 1683 Pennsylvania required that all children learn to read and learn skills to support themselves, but this law was not enforced (Cremin, 1970). In the Spanish pueblos of California, free schooling began to be available in 1794. In 1847, the San Francisco Town Council built a one-room schoolhouse where education was free for indigent children (Lascarides & Hinitz, 2000). In 1779 Thomas Jefferson proposed to the Virginia legislature his Bill for the More General Diffusion of Knowledge, which called for a three-tiered system of education that began with 3 years of free elementary education for White males and females in reading, writing, and arithmetic (Cremin, 1970). While this bill was not passed, by the 1870s Virginia and most other states were willing to commit themselves to tax-supported systems of public schools (Lascarides & Hinitz, 2000). As Cremin observes,

> The fight for free schools was a bitter one. . . . The tide of education reform flowed in one state, only to ebb in another. Legislation passed one year was sometimes repealed the next. State laws requiring public schools were ignored by the local communities that were supposed to build them. . . . Yet by 1860 a design had begun to appear. . . . A majority of the states had established public school systems, and a good half of the nation's children were already getting some formal education. (1961, p. 13)

Equal Access for Diverse Populations to an Appropriate Education

Prior to the establishment of free public schooling, access to education was vastly inequitable. As shown in Table 2.1, we estimate that in 1850, only 2% of African-American and other children of color ages 5 to 19 were enrolled in school, compared to 56% of White students. After the Civil War, the percent-

TABLE 2.1. Percentage of 5- to 19-Year-Olds in School

Year	Total	White	Black and Other
1850	47.2	56.2	1.8
1860	50.6	59.6	1.9
1870	48.4	54.4	9.9
1880	57.8	62.0	33.8
1890	54.3	57.9	32.9
1900	50.5	53.6	31.1
1910	59.2	61.3	44.8
1920	64.3	65.7	53.5
1930	69.9	71.2	60.3
1940	74.8	75.6	68.4
1950	78.7	79.3	74.8
1960	88.6	89.0	86.1
1970	90.6	90.8	89.4
1980	89.1	88.9	90.4
1989	91.8	91.7	92.1

Source: U.S. Department of Education (1993)

age of minority students in school rose to 10%, and climbed sharply to 34% by 1880. White and minority populations were not enrolled in school in comparable percentages until 1970 (U.S. Department of Education, 1993).

Even after most children gained access to school, the quality of educational experiences remained inequitable across groups. By the middle of the 20th century, "American public education was not a seamless system of roughly similar common schools but instead a diverse and unequal set of institutions that reflected deeply embedded economic and social inequalities" (Tyack & Cuban, 1995, p. 22). Urban and Wagoner (2000) demonstrate the glaring inequities in literacy rates, per pupil expenditures, and teacher salaries in Southern states in the first part of the 20th century for White students and staff as compared with their Black counterparts. In the latter half of the 20th century, protest movements emerged that "developed a new style of activist reform and could take much of the credit for desegregation in the South, new attention to the children of immigrants, attacks on discriminatory gender practices, and better education of children with special needs" (Tyack & Cuban, 1995, p. 26). The Supreme Court's 1954 *Brown v. Board of Education* decision ordering schools to racially integrate inspired activism on behalf of other groups of underserved children. Court decisions and subsequent legislation have enshrined principles of equity in law, but U.S. society continues to struggle with providing equitable services and producing equitable outcomes for children regardless of socioeconomic status. "Public schools are one of the few American institutions that try to take equality seriously. Yet their service in this cause has been ambiguous and frequently compromised, for the schools are a public institution oriented to equality in a society dominated by private institutions oriented to the market" (Cohen & Neufeld, 1981, as cited in Tyack & Cuban, 1995, p. 29). In the past century, services for preschool-age children have been far more vulnerable to market forces than public education, with resulting inequalities of quality and even availability (Ranck, 2003).

Efforts to Make School Compulsory

In 1837 the Massachusetts legislature passed An Act Relating to Common Schools, establishing a state board of education (Lascarides & Hinitz, 2000). Horace Mann, in his lecture "Means and Objects of Common School Education," asserted, "Education must be universal. . . . With us, the qualification of voters is as important as the qualification of governors, and even comes first, in the natural order" (Mann, 1855, p. 55). He promoted the idea of the rich and poor being educated together as defining the character of America (Lascarides & Hinitz, 2000; Mann, 1855). Political support for compulsory school grew with industrialization, both in response to working parents leaving children unsupervised and to protect children from child labor. Political opposition came from a general opposition to government compulsion, and sometimes from families who relied on the labor of their children, such as farmers (Urban & Wagoner, 2000). In 1852 Massachusetts was the first state to pass a compulsory school attendance law; in 1918 Mississippi was the last state to initiate compulsory school attendance (Lascarides & Hinitz, 2000).

The age at which school becomes compulsory is determined by the individual states and ranges from age 5 to age 8 (Cryer & Clifford, 2003). Kindergarten[1] enrollment is mandated in the District of Columbia and seven states: Arkansas, Delaware, Maryland, New Mexico, Oklahoma, South Carolina, and Virginia. All states require children to attend school until they are at least 16 years old, and in several states school remains compulsory until age 17 or 18 (U.S. Department of Education, 2005a).

Early Examples of Voluntary Education for Young Children

"There is every indication that the number of schools and the extent of schooling increased markedly during the eighteenth century and that it increased more rapidly than the increase in population" (Cremin, 1970, p. 500). This increase comprised a variety of forms of instruction and institutions, serving children of a range of ages. The expansion of voluntary schooling to younger children in the 18th and 19th centuries was driven in part by the needs of industrial employers and their workers, and also by philosophical movements. Many infant schools were established between 1700 and 1840 for the children of factory workers, in some cases supported by the factories themselves and in some cases by social service organizations. These schools fell out of favor in the mid-19th century, with a movement to promote children's care at home (Lascarides & Hinitz, 2000). Older children attended school in greater numbers as factories mechanized and there were fewer opportunities for child labor. Younger children went to school with older siblings when mothers worked; teachers feared that if the young were turned away, the older siblings would have had to go with them (Whitbread, 1972).

Individual educators and social reformers promoted kindergarten and the philosophies of Pestalozzi and Froebel. Robert Owen established an infant school and the first U.S. kindergarten in 1824, in New Harmony, Indiana (Lascarides & Hinitz, 2000). Between 1850 and 1870 German immigrants established kindergartens in a number of communities. Articles were published in the 1850s about the philosophy and practices of kindergarten. These ideas were not immediately embraced by U.S. society because education was seen as instruction in the three Rs (reading, writing, and arithmetic) (Vandewalker, 1908). Elizabeth Palmer Peabody promoted kindergarten in the 1860s and 1870s, visiting Europe to clarify her ideas, and influenced the U.S. Bureau of Education to publish a *Circular of Information on the Kindergarten* in 1872. From 1873 to 1875 she published the *Kindergarten Messenger*, with articles such as "The Relation of the Kindergarten to the Primary School." This publication was an important forum for the propagation of kindergarten (for example, in the South for children of all colors). In 1876 the *Kindergarten Messenger* became a section of the *New England Journal of Education* (Lascarides & Hinitz, 2000).

Public Kindergartens

While the U.S. kindergarten movement gained swift momentum in the 1870s, in general kindergarten was deemed to belong to the private sphere rather than the public sphere. "Americans were ready to accept the idea of privately controlled extrafamilial education for young children but not the extension of public schooling to children under the age of six" (Beatty, 1995, p. 53). In the 19th century kindergarten began to be incorporated into public school in some Midwestern states. German immigrants in St. Louis, Missouri, established neighborhood kindergartens that were ultimately incorporated into public schools (Troen, 1975). "By 1876, St. Louis provided a national model for the operation and management of kindergartens, and for training kindergarten teachers" (Lascarides & Hinitz, 2000). Kindergarten gained popularity as a transitional year for children before first grade, and by the end of the 20th century was firmly established in public and private elementary schools.

CURRENT POLICIES AND PRACTICES

Present-day governance and funding of schools is still strongly influenced by decisions made by the founders of the Republic. The delegates to the Constitutional Convention signed a constitution in 1787 that did not mention education. The founders of the United States had struggled for months to craft a document that balanced the Federalist principles of some delegates with the urgent efforts of many others to preserve the rights of individual states to govern within their own borders, believing that "state governments offered the chief protection for personal liberties" (Bruns, 1986). Founders such as Benjamin Rush and Thomas Jefferson were eloquent proponents of publicly supported education as essential to the success of democracy, and "seven of the fourteen states that had joined the Union by 1800 had made explicit in their constitutions state responsibility for education. In time all states were to do so" (Urban & Wagoner, 2000, p. 81). Therefore, in the 21st century, state and local governments continue to fund and regulate education, with some federal involvement. There remains, particularly for younger children, a strong private-sector role.

In the United States we have experienced an ongoing evolution in the population served in public school settings. In 1954, in the historic *Brown v. Board of Education* case, the U.S. Supreme Court ruled that separate schools for children of different races were inherently unequal, permitting enforcement of more equitable access to schools. With the adoption of the Education of the Handicapped Act in the 1960s and subsequent revisions of that law, Congress mandated that children with disabilities be included as a part of the regular school population. Some one million children who had previously been excluded from school due to disabilities entered the system, and schools were eventually mandated to serve children under age 5 with disabilities. During roughly this same period of time, public schools gradually increased the number of children offered kindergarten. In the United States today, most states mandate that children are eligible for publicly supported kindergarten at about age 5. By 2005, some 3.9 million children (equivalent to roughly 99% of 5-year-olds) were enrolled in kindergarten (U.S. Census Bureau, 2006), even though in most states school is not compulsory for children until at least age 6 (U.S. Department of Education, 2005b).

The care and education of children from birth to age 5 have received increasing public funding and attention. During the last half of the 20th century, the United States experienced a major shift in women's participation in the paid labor force. By the year 2000, 63% of all women with children under the age of 6 were actively employed in the paid labor force. This was up from only about 12% in 1950 (Blau & Currie, 2004). One of the results of this shift was a dramatic rise in the provision of nonparental child care for children under age 6 and increasing pressure on state and federal governments to provide support for such care. While not their primary purpose, public schools had for a long time had a secondary role of providing care for children starting at age 5 or 6 that enabled mothers to enter the paid labor force. This was evidenced by the fact that prior to the 1960s women were unlikely to enter the labor force until their youngest child entered school (Fullerton, 1999). As the country experienced this shift in working patterns among mothers of children under age 6 and the resulting major increase in the need for care for these children, private nonprofit and for-profit entities met most of the demand, with parent fees typically covering most of the cost. The public schools, however, increasingly fill part of this need. The large percentage of children needing care combined with new information on the extent of learning that occurs prior to age 6, highlighted by what has become known as "brain research," have brought increased public funding as well as public oversight to the diverse community of public and private providers of early care and education.

Children Age 3 to 5

Child care and nursery schools gained greater public support in the 1960s and 1970s as a result of the War on Poverty and the dramatically increased labor force participation of women, particularly middle-class women (Cryer & Clifford, 2003). At that time, the Head Start program was established to provide health and education services to poor children, and Congress enacted the first child care legislation (Cryer & Clifford, 2003). Efforts were made to limit the scope of these programs and to ensure that the private sector would continue to play a large role in providing services. Education programs for children ages 3 to 5 are provided by for-profit companies, private nonprofit organizations, and government agencies and may be supported by federal, state, and local funding streams, in addition to parent fees and private donations. Even when federal dollars are used and federal regulations apply to programs, "states and local communities traditionally play an extensive role in the distribution, planning, and development of new child care, early education, and school-age [after-school] programs" (Children's Defense Fund, 2004, p. 1).

Settings and Number of Children Served. In 2002, 12.5 million of the 18.5 million children under age 5 (68%) were in some form of regular non-parental child care arrangement during a typical week. Thirty-two percent were cared for by a relative other than a parent, and 35% by a non-relative (Overturf Johnson, 2005). Non-relative care might include care in the child's home or the provider's home, or in a facility such as a child care center or Head Start program. Increasingly, children under 5 are being served by public schools. In 2001, 867,000 children were enrolled in public school–based pre-kindergarten; 3.4 million children were enrolled in public kindergarten (U.S. Department of Education,

2004). Pre-kindergarten enrollment of 3- to 5-year-olds rose by 20% between 1991 and 2001 (U.S. Department of Education, 2004). Thirty-five percent of public elementary schools had pre-kindergarten programs in 2000–2001 (Wirt et al., 2004).

Settings and Characteristics of Children and Programs. States license child care centers and family child care homes; each state sets its own standards and there is substantial variation in those standards from state to state. For example, states vary in their maximum child/staff ratios, from 8:1 for 4-year-olds in New York to 20:1 in North Carolina (Children's Defense Fund, 2004). States are working to raise quality through initiatives such as star-rated license programs, but these systems still allow for variation within states as well as between them. One exception is the federal program Head Start, which demands that all of its funded classrooms meet certain standards. Voluntary accreditation is available to other early childhood care and education programs, for example by the National Association for the Education of Young Children (NAEYC).

The United States is a diverse society, and various social and cultural factors seem to play a role in the choices families make about care and education for their young children, as well as in the range of options available to families. Blau and Currie found ethnic differences in use of types of care, with Black mothers more likely to use care from relatives or child care centers and less likely to use non-relative care, while Hispanic mothers are most likely to use relative care and least likely to use centers (2004). In addition, Hispanic mothers have been found to use care by a sibling or other relative (19%) twice as often as non-Hispanic White mothers (8%) (Overturf Johnson, 2005). Family income and education are also related to choices of types of service used. Children living in families whose incomes are below the federal poverty guideline are less likely to be enrolled in center-based early care and education programs than children in families whose incomes are at or above the poverty guideline (47% vs. 60%), while children whose mothers had completed college attended center-based programs 73% of the time compared to 35% of children whose mothers had less than a high school education (U.S. Department of Education, 2007).

Head Start classrooms serve low-income families, and are federally funded and monitored. State, territory, and tribal governments contribute additional funds in some cases; local grantees administer programs in their communities. Grantees may be local school districts or other local government agencies, or private nonprofit organizations. In 2004, 115 Head Start and Early Head Start programs were sponsored by faith-based organizations (U.S. Department of Health and Human Services, 2005). As state and local school districts have begun and expanded pre-kindergarten programs serving primarily 4-year-old children, Head Start has gradually begun serving more 3-year-olds. In 2004, 52% of the children in Head Start programs were 4 years old; 34% were 3. The population of children is quite diverse, with 31.2% Hispanic, 31.1% African-American, 26.9% White, 3.1% American Indian/Alaska native, 1.8% Asian, 0.9% Hawaiian/Pacific Islander, and 5% other/multiracial (U.S. Department of Health and Human Services, 2005). The Head Start program traditionally takes a holistic approach to bettering the lives of children, providing health as well as education services, and focusing heavily on parent empowerment. In 2004, 27% of Head Start staff were parents of current or former Head Start children (U.S. Department of Health and Human Services, 2005).

Federal Funding. In FY 2004, $6.5 billion in federal funds were spent for local Head Start projects, and $241 million for support activities (U.S. Department of Health and Human Services, 2005). The average expenditure per child was $7,222; 905,851 children were served. Title I is another source of federal funding that can be used to provide preschool education or to improve educational quality for disadvantaged children. Funds are disbursed to public schools serving a high concentration of disadvantaged families. Unlike Head Start, Title I is administered by the U.S. Department of Education.

The Individuals with Disabilities Education Act (IDEA) funds pre-primary service through grants for preschool classes for children with disabilities aged 3 to 5. States, territories, and tribes also receive grants to provide services for families of children with disabilities aged birth to 3 (Cryer & Clifford, 2003). In 2000–2001, 5% of U.S. preschoolers (599,678) received some IDEA services (U.S. Department of Education, 2001).

Child care subsidies are available to some families based on financial need. Federal grants are supplied to states, territories, and tribes through the Child Care and Development Fund; families may apply for funds to offset or cover the cost of private child care or fees that may be associated with publicly supported programs. "Only one out of seven eligible children under federal law actually receives child care assistance" (Children's Defense Fund, 2004, p. 1). States vary greatly in the maximum income they allow to qualify for a subsidy and in the amount of parent co-pay (Children's Defense Fund, 2004). The Child Care and Development Fund is a source of federal dollars that states have some flexibility in allocating for quality improvement and research. In fiscal year 2006, $5 billion in federal funds were available to states, territories, and tribes through this program (U.S. Department of Health and Human Services, 2006). The average subsidy payment for center-based care for 4- to 5-year-olds was $416 per month ($4,992 per year) in 2005 (U.S. Department of Health and Human Services, 2007).

The Dependent Care Tax Credit and Child and Dependent Care Tax Credit both provide a federal tax offset to families paying for child care. In 2001 the total for these two tax credits was about $1.9 billion (Barnett & Masse, 2003). These credits are provided directly to individual families and cannot be combined. Most states also have either a tax credit or deduction in place that can be claimed in addition to the federal credit (Children's Defense Fund, 2004).

State Funding. While continuing to fund child care subsidies for low-income children and special education services, states are increasingly funding and overseeing pre-kindergarten programs. The programs are supported in some states by lotteries and court settlements from lawsuits against tobacco companies. A majority of states are now providing pre-kindergarten programs for some 4-year-olds, and in some cases 3-year-olds as well. Over $3.3 billion is being spent on these programs (Barnett, Hustedt, Hawkinson, & Robin, 2006). In some states these programs are provided in public schools; in most a mix of private and public settings are used.

Local Funding. School districts may support programs for pre-kindergarten children by contributing funds, administrative support, or space, or by paying part or all of the total costs from local funds. Schools may house or operate programs funded by Head Start, Title I, IDEA, state funds, district funds, parent fees, or any combination of those sources.

Private child care is largely supported by a combination of parent fees and government subsidies provided directly to families or to the child care providers. Private child care providers may also receive cash or in-kind contributions from charitable organizations or businesses, thereby reducing the financial burden on families. A few employers provide child care for employees through either a subsidy-of-costs arrangement or by directly providing the child care service and paying for all or a major part of the costs for this service as a benefit to the employee.

Regulation. Child care regulations are set by states, tribes, and territories, not the federal government, with the exception of Head Start. "The federal government can impose standards that child care providers must meet in order to be eligible for federal subsidies, but the federal government is not authorized to regulate child care" (Blau & Currie, 2004, p. 35). States regulate structural features such as ratios and group size, monitor health and safety, and, increasingly, offer incentives to increase quality.

Teacher Education. All states that regulate early childhood programs require some type of education for teachers, either preservice or inservice. A few don't require any particular training (Children's Defense Fund, 2004). However, there is a movement to promote higher levels of formal education among child care teachers. Accreditation of child care programs by NAEYC was recently revised to include higher expectations for teacher qualifications. Now, in order for a program to be accredited by NAEYC, most teachers will need to hold a Child Development Associate credential (CDA) or its equivalent, or be working toward an associate's degree (a 2-year postsecondary degree, a lower degree than a bachelor's degree) (NAEYC, 2007).

Many states require higher levels of education for teachers in their pre-kindergarten classrooms. A recent study of pre-kindergarten in 11 states found that 73% of lead teachers had a bachelor's degree or more. Another 12% had associate's degrees (Early et al., 2005). In the 2005–2006 school year, 18 of the 38 state pre-kindergarten programs required every teacher to have at least a bachelor's degree. Of the remaining states, eight required some teachers to have a bachelor's degree and eight had no requirements for a bachelor's degree (Barnett et al., 2006). But as can be seen from the findings from the pre-K study cited above, the trend is clearly toward having a bachelor's degree as the standard for pre-kindergarten teachers.

Children Age 5 to 8

Most children in the United States attend public schools, beginning with kindergarten, at age 5. A significant number do attend private and parochial school—11.3% of 6- to 11-year-olds in 2000 (U.S. Census Bureau, 2006). A small but increasing number are educated at home by their parents. In 2003, 2.2% of children age 5 to 17 were home-schooled, and the reasons for this choice reflect some persistent themes in U.S. education. Thirty-one percent of parents reported that their most important reason for home-schooling was concern about the environment of other schools; 30% said their most important reason was to provide religious or moral instruction; 17% were dissatisfied with the academic instruction at other schools (U.S. Department of Education, 2005a).

Characteristics of Children and Classrooms. Ninety-two percent of 5-year-olds were enrolled in school in 2003; most children now attend kindergarten for a full school day (65%) (Shin, 2005). In 2002, student/teacher ratio in public schools was estimated at 16.1; in private schools, 16.2. The average class size in public elementary schools was 21.1 (U.S. Department of Education, 2004).

The population of children in schools is becoming increasingly diverse. In 1992, 64.8% of 1st graders were White; in 2004, 55.4% were White. Hispanic students have now overtaken African-American students as the largest minority group (U.S. Department of Education, 2006a). It is projected that by 2025 there will be no majority race in schools (Hodgkinson, 2000).

Funding. Like education for children under age 5, public K–12 education is also supported by federal, state, and local funding streams. In 2000–2001, the state share of revenues for public schools was 49.7%; the local share was 43.1%; and the federal share was 7.3% (U.S. Department of Education, 2004). Parents provide lunches, though children from low- and moderate-income families may receive free or reduced-price school lunches through the National School Lunch Program (U.S. Department of Agriculture, 2006). Parents typically also provide some school supplies, and may be charged a small fee for special activities.

Expenditures per student have risen sharply since World War II, from an average of $800 (in 1989–1990 dollars) in 1939–1940 to $4,960 in 1989–1990 (U.S. Department of Education, 1993). By 2003–2004, median current expenditures[2] per pupil in membership by district averaged $7,860 across states, but the amount of funding varies enormously by state and by district within states (see Table 2.2; U.S. Department of Education, 2006b).

School-Age Aftercare. The typical primary school day is not as long as the workday of many parents (Blau & Currie, 2004). Children may spend time before or after the regular school day in "wraparound" or "after" care. This care may be provided by the school, typically for a fee, or in a separate setting. Low-income parents may qualify for a government subsidy for aftercare. Sixty-three percent of children ages 5 to 14 of employed mothers

> regularly spend time in some form of non-school, non-parental care, compared to 31 percent of children of non-employed mothers. Children of employed mothers spend an average of 22 to 30 hours a week in such arrangements. . . . Two-thirds to three-quarters of these activities involve a monetary payment. (Blau & Currie, 2004, p. 3)

Most primary schools still have a summer break of several weeks, though increasing numbers of schools operate on a year-round schedule with shorter breaks several times a year. The National Association for Year-Round Education estimates that about 4% of K–12 students attend a year-round school (2007). Capizzano, Adelman, and Stagner (2002) found that during the summer, 27% of 6- to 9-year-old children are in at least one child care arrangement that can be defined as an organized program (a summer program, summer school, or a before- and/or after-school program), 44% spend time with a relative, and 12% are in family child care or with a nanny or babysitter. One percent spend some time in charge of themselves.

TABLE 2.2. Selected States' Expenditures per Public School Pupil

State	State median	5th percentile (school district)	95th percentile (school district)
Alaska	$14,667	$7,643	$23,491
Utah	$5,862	$4,558	$11,158
New York	$12,421	$9,837	$19,286

Source: U.S. Department of Education, 2006b

Regulation. As stated earlier in this chapter, the U.S. Constitution does not list education as a federal responsibility, reserving governance of education for the various states. In recent decades the federal government has intervened in public education, but most prominently in its role of protecting the rights of various populations of children (e.g., children with disabilities). However, public schools are still primarily regulated by states and, through state delegation of authority, by districts within states. Governance varies by state and may include state-level legislative committees; a state board of education, which may include elected members and members appointed by the governor of the state; regional boards and superintendents; and local boards and superintendents. Local school board members may be directly elected by the citizens of the district, or may be appointed by elected city or county officials. Some states have policies in place that allow for collective bargaining by teachers and staff, while others do not (Education Commission of the States, 2007). See Table 2.3 for a comparison of Connecticut's and North Carolina's governance structures.

TRANSFORMING PRE-KINDERGARTEN EDUCATION

Major changes in family social and economic life occurred during the second half of the 20th century in the United States. These changes included an increasing reliance on women, including women with young children, to provide a major portion of the family income (Blau & Currie, 2004). In 1950, 33.9% of women age 16 and older were in the paid workforce; by 1998, 59.8% were (Fullerton, 1999). By the turn of the century, more than half of all women were in the paid workforce within a year of having a baby (Dye, 2005). Workforce participation rates for mothers with preschoolers are even higher, with the vast majority of children spending some time in out-of-home care and education prior to kindergarten (Overturf Johnson, 2005).

Public officials were slow to recognize this shift in family life as being a lasting change, so public policies have lagged far behind the needs of families. But by the 1990s we began to see significant efforts on the part of government to adjust to the new demands on families and to seek means of supporting the new realities (Kamerman & Gatenio, 2003). The initial response was to expect the market to respond to demand, and indeed there was a very large increase in the provision of out-of-home child care that coincided with the increased female participation in the paid workforce (Kamerman & Gatenio, 2003). However, as pointed out in the Cost, Quality and Child Outcomes in Child Care Centers study, market forces worked to increase the supply of child care and to hold down the cost to families at the expense of the quality of services to children in care (Cost, Quality and Child Outcomes Study Team, 1995). As it became

TABLE 2.3. State Comparisons: K–12 Governance Structures in Connecticut and North Carolina

	Connecticut	North Carolina
Legislature	The legislature has a joint education committee.	The legislature has a house education committee, a senate education/higher education committee, a senate appropriations committee on education/higher education, and a joint legislative oversight committee.
Governor	The governor appoints all of the voting members of the state board of education.	The governor appoints 11 of the 13 voting members of the state board of education and 3 non-voting members of the state board of education (one high school junior, one high school senior, and one local superintendent).
Chief State School Officer	The chief state school officer is appointed by the state board of education.	The chief state school officer is elected.
State Board of Education	There are 9 voting members of the state board of education. All of the voting members are appointed by the governor. The commissioner of higher education serves as an ex-officio, non-voting member and 2 students serve as non-voting members.	There are 13 voting members of the state board of education. Eleven of the 13 members are appointed by the governor. Two of the 13 voting members, the lieutenant governor and state treasurer, are elected. The lieutenant governor and state treasurer also are ex-officio members. The teacher of the year, the principal of the year, and one local school board member are ex-officio, non-voting members. One high school junior, one high school senior, and one local superintendent are non-voting members.
Regional Boards	There are 6 regional educational service center boards. Members of regional school boards are appointed by participating local school boards.	There are no regional boards.

	Connecticut	North Carolina
Regional Superintendents	There are 6 regional educational service center directors. Regional educational service center directors are appointed by regional educational service center boards.	There are no regional superintendents.
Local School Boards	There are 169 local school boards and regional school boards. Local school board members and regional school board members are elected.	There are 117 local school boards. There are city school boards and county school boards. Members of 14 city school boards and 100 county school boards are elected, and members of 3 city school boards are appointed by city councils.
Local Superintendents	There are 169 local superintendents and regional superintendents. Local superintendents are appointed by local school boards, and regional superintendents are appointed by regional school boards.	There are 117 local superintendents. There are city superintendents and county superintendents. Local superintendents are appointed by local school boards.
Public Schools	There are 1,075 public schools.	There are 2,158 public schools.
Collective Bargaining Agreements	There is a state policy that allows collective bargaining for teachers.	There is not a state policy that allows collective bargaining for teachers.

increasingly evident that low-quality care in the early years of life had long-term negative consequences for children and ultimately for society, officials began to invest increasing amounts of government resources in services for children (Blau & Currie, 2004).

Initial investments were in the form of subsidies to pay for private child care for low-income working families (Barnett & Masse, 2003; Blau & Currie, 2004). Government regulation of child care has largely been left to states, with minimal efforts at the federal level to ensure that the care was beneficial for young children (Azer, Morgan, Clifford, & Crawford, 2002). Gradually, emphasis has shifted toward a greater interest in the impact of early childhood services on children's later success in school and specifically on cognitive development. States have moved to launch new programs to serve 4-year-old children and some 3-year-old children in pre-kindergarten programs that are linked to the education system. Currently, about 80% of all states have a state-funded pre-kindergarten program in place (Barnett et al., 2006). Most states target children who are at risk of school failure, but there is ongoing debate about providing universal access to these pre-kindergarten programs, at least for 4-year-olds. Now nearly a million children are in these state-funded programs, a number equal to about one-fourth of all 4-year-olds in the United States. A total of 26 of the 38 state pre-K programs include 3-year-olds; however, overall only about 3% of 3-year-olds (or about 120,000 children) are now in state preschool programs, and a total of 14% (530,000 children) when Head Start and preschool special education programs are included (Barnett et al., 2006). The fact that so many states have included 3-year-olds in their program does suggest that schools may eventually extend services to this population on a wider basis. It is impossible to tell at this point whether schools will extend services to even younger children in the foreseeable future.

Along with the investment of education resources has come an increasing role for public schools in the delivery of services to children this age. While most states also allow private groups to operate pre-kindergarten classes as part of the state pre-K program as long as they agree to abide by program and personnel standards, public elementary schools are playing a major new role in serving children at earlier and earlier ages. Overall, about half of all state-funded pre-K classes are in public schools (Early et al., 2005). This trend is indicative of a major shift toward increasing public involvement in education for children under 5, at both the federal and state level, not only in terms of funding and governance but also in the delivery of service.

As shown through the information presented in this chapter, the United States has witnessed major changes in the education of young children over the past half-century. We have moved from a situation in which the majority of children under the age of 6 were at home with one or more parents to a situation in which nearly all 5-year-olds are in either a public or private kindergarten and a majority of 4-year-olds are in either a pre-kindergarten or a child care center. Increasingly, 3-year-olds are in similar non-parental group settings. These settings are in a much wider variety of organizations than services for children ages 5 to 18, which are largely provided by public schools. Services for children under age 5 are often in private settings, including both nonprofit and for-profit organizations. There is a strong movement to increase the participation of public schools, and to more formally link these childhood services with primary school operation (see Chapter 1 for a discussion of some of the ramifications of this movement).

NOTES

1. In the United States, kindergarten is offered by almost all public and private elementary schools for children who attain the age of 5 by a specified date. For most families it is the first year of free public education.

2. Excludes capital outlay and interest on school debt.

REFERENCES

Azer, S., Morgan, G., Clifford, R. M., & Crawford, G. M. (2002). Regulation of child care. *Early Childhood Research & Policy Briefs, 2*(1). National Center for Early Development and Learning, Chapel Hill, NC.

Barnett, W. S., Hustedt, J. T., Hawkinson, L. E., & Robin, K. B. (2006). *The state of preschool: 2006 state preschool yearbook.* New Brunswick, NJ: National Institute for Early Education Research.

Barnett, W. S., & Masse, L. N. (2003). Funding issues for early childhood education and care programs. In D. Cryer & R. Clifford (Eds.), *Early childhood education & care in the USA* (pp. 137–165). Baltimore: Paul H. Brookes.

Beatty, B. (1995). *Preschool education in America: The culture of young children from the colonial era to the present.* New Haven, CT: Yale University Press.

Blau, D., & Currie, J. (2004). *Preschool, day care, and afterschool care: Who's minding the kids?* (Working paper number 10670). Cambridge, MA: National Bureau of Economic Research. Retrieved September 28, 2005, from http://www.nber.org/papers/w10670

Bruns, A. R. (1986) *A more perfect union: The creation of the U.S. Constitution.* Washington, DC: Published for the National Archives and Records Administration by the National Archives Trust Fund Board. Retrieved January 19, 2007, from http://www.archives.gov/national-archives-experience/charters/constitution_history.html

Capizzano, J., Adelman, S., & Stagner, M. (2002, June). *What happens when the school year is over? The use and costs of child care for school-age children during the summer months* (Assessing the New Federalism, Occasional Paper Number 58). Washington, DC: Urban Institute.

Children's Defense Fund. (2004). *State developments in child care, early education, and school-age care: 2003.* Washington, DC: Author.

Cost, Quality and Child Outcomes Study Team. (1995). *Cost, quality, and child outcomes in child care centers.* Denver: University of Colorado, Center for Research in Economics and Social Policy, Department of Economics.

Cremin, L. A. (1961). *The transformation of the school: Progressivism in American education, 1876–1957.* New York: Knopf.

Cremin, L. A. (1970). *American education: The colonial experience.* New York: Harper & Row.

Cryer, D., & Clifford, R. (Eds.). (2003). *Early childhood education & care in the USA.* Baltimore: Paul H. Brookes.

Dye, J. L. (2005). *Fertility of American women: June 2004.* Current Population Survey P20-555, U.S. Census Bureau. Retrieved July 12, 2006, from http://www.census.gov/prod/2005pubs/p20-555.pdf

Early, D., Barbarin, O., Bryant, D., Burchinal, M., Chang, F., Clifford, R., Crawford, G., Weaver, W., Howes, C., Ritchie, R., Kraft-Sayre, M., Pianta, R., & Barnett, W. (2005). *Pre-kindergarten in eleven states: NCEDL's multi-state study of pre-kindergarten & study of state-wide early education programs (SWEEP): Preliminary descriptive report* (NCEDL Working Paper). Chapel Hill: University of North Carolina. Retrieved December 29, 2006, from http://www.fpg.unc.edu/~ncedl/pdfs/SWEEP_MS_summary_final.pdf

Education Commission of the States. (2007). K–12 governance online database. Retrieved November 6, 2007, from http://www.ecs.org/html/educationIssues/Governance/GovK12DB_intro.asp

Fullerton, H. N. (1999, December). Labor force participation: 75 years of change, 1950–98 and 1998–2025. *Monthly Labor Review*, pp. 3–12. Retrieved June 19, 2007, from http://www.bls.gov/opub/mlr/1999/12/art1full.pdf

Hodgkinson, H. (2000). *Secondary schools in a new millennium: Demographic certainties, social realities*. Reston, VA: National Association of Secondary School Principals.

Kamerman, S. B., & Gatenio, S. (2003). Overview of the current policy context. In D. Cryer & R. Clifford (Eds.), *Early childhood education & care in the USA* (pp. 1–30). Baltimore: Paul H. Brookes.

Lascarides, V. C., & Hinitz, B. (2000). *History of early childhood education*. New York: Falmer.

Mann, H. (1855). *Lectures on education*. Boston: Ide & Dutton.

National Association for the Education of Young Children. (2007, March). Education qualifications of program administrators and teachers staff: Building better futures for children and the profession. *Beyond the Journal: Young Children on the Web*. Retrieved June 19, 2007, from http://journal.naeyc.org/btj/200703/pdf/BTJProfDev.pdf

National Association for Year-Round Education. (2007). *Statistical summaries of year-round education programs: 2006–2007*. San Diego, CA: Author. Retrieved July 18, 2007, from http://www.nayre.org/STATISTICAL%20SUMMARIES%20OF%20YRE%202007.pdf

Overturf Johnson, J. (2005). *Who's minding the kids? Child care arrangements: Winter 2002*. (Current Population Reports, P70-101). Washington, DC: U.S. Census Bureau.

Ranck, E. R. (2003). Access to programs. In D. Cryer & R. Clifford (Eds.), *Early childhood education & care in the USA* (pp. 47–63). Baltimore: Paul H. Brookes.

Shin, H. B. (2005). *School enrollment: Social and economic characteristics of students: October 2003* (Current Population Reports, P20–554). Washington, DC: U.S. Census Bureau.

Troen, S. K. (1975). *The public and the schools: Shaping the St. Louis system, 1838–1920*. Columbia: University of Missouri Press.

Tyack, D., & Cuban, L. (1995). *Tinkering toward Utopia: A century of public school reform*. Cambridge, MA: Harvard University Press.

Urban, W. J., & Wagoner, J. L. (2000). *American education: A history* (2nd ed.). Boston: McGraw-Hill.

U.S. Census Bureau. (2006). *Current population survey, October 2005*. Internet release date December 19, 2006. http://www.census.gov/population/www/socdemo/school/cps2005.html

U.S. Department of Agriculture. (2006). *National school lunch program fact sheet*. Washington, DC: Author. Retrieved June 19, 2007, from http://www.fns.usda.gov/cnd/lunch/AboutLunch/NSLPFactSheet.pdf

U.S. Department of Education. (2001). *Twenty-fourth annual report to Congress on the implementation of the Individuals with Disabilities Education Act*. Washington, DC: Author.

U.S. Department of Education, National Center for Education Statistics. (1993). *120 years of American education: A statistical portrait.* Washington, DC: U.S. Government Printing Office.

U.S. Department of Education, National Center for Education Statistics. (2004).*Digest of education statistics, 2003.* Washington, DC: Author.

U.S. Department of Education, National Center for Education Statistics. (2005a). *The condition of education 2005* (NCES 2005-094). Washington, DC: U.S. Government Printing Office.

U.S. Department of Education, National Center for Education Statistics. (2005b). *Digest of education statistics, 2004.* Washington, DC: Author.

U.S. Department of Education, National Center for Education Statistics. (2006a). *Common core of data* [data file]. Retrieved October 30, 2006, from http://nces.ed.gov/ccd/bat/

U.S. Department of Education, National Center for Education Statistics. (2006b). *Current expenditures for public elementary and secondary education: School year 2003–04* (NCES 2006-352). Washington, DC: U.S. Government Printing Office.

U.S. Department of Education, National Center for Education Statistics. (2007). *The condition of education 2007* (NCES 2007-064). Washington, DC: U.S. Government Printing Office.

U.S. Department of Health and Human Services, Administration for Children and Families. (2005). *2005 Head Start fact sheet.* Washington, DC: Author. Retrieved September 28, 2005, from http://www2.acf.dhhs.gov/programs/hsb/research/2005.htm

U.S. Department of Health and Human Services, Administration for Children and Families. (2006). *Child Care and Development Fund fact sheet, October 2006.* Washington, DC: Author. Retrieved July 18, 2007, from http://www.acf.hhs.gov/programs/ccb/ccdf/factsheet.htm

U.S. Department of Health and Human Services, Administration for Children and Families. (2007). *FFY 2005 CCDF Data Tables, final data June 2007.* Washington, DC: Author. Retrieved July 18, 2007, from http://www.acf.hhs.gov/programs/ccb/data/ccdf_data/05acf800/table15.htm

Vandewalker, N. C. (1908). *The kindergarten in American education.* New York: Macmillan.

Whitbread, N. (1972). *The evolution of the nursery-infant school: A history of infant and nursery education in Britain, 1800–1970.* London: Routledge & Kegan Paul.

Wirt, J., Choy, S., Rooney, P., Provasnik, S., Sen, A., & Tobin, R. (2004). *The condition of education 2004* (NCES 2004-077). (U.S. Department of Education, National Center for Education Statistics). Washington, DC: U.S. Government Printing Office.

CHAPTER 3

French Primary Schools
History and Identity

VÉRONIQUE FRANCIS

Since the 19th century, French *écoles primaires* (primary schools) have been divided into two systems: *école maternelle* and elementary school. École maternelle is for children between the ages of 2 and 6. After this period, children will attend elementary school and, at about age 11, they will move up to *collège,* which is the same as junior high school in the United States.

Within the école maternelle system, there are several classes organized around pupils' ages. The youngest ones (ages 2 to 3) attend the lower age group, level one, the smallest section (*toute petite section*). Children age 3 to 4 attend the lower group, level two, small section class (*petite section*). Children age 4 to 5 are in the medium group, level three (*moyenne section*). Children age 5 to 6 attend the upper age group (*grande section*).

The school year runs from September to July. However, school attendance depends on the calendar year of birth. Thus, children attending the youngest section at the beginning of the 2008–2009 school year are born between January 1 and December 31, 2006. Class management is connected with the organization of école maternelle. Groups are made up according to the ages of the children. It is possible that pedagogical decisions of the teaching staff lead to multi-age classes.

Since the 1989 Educational Guidance Law, *Loi d'orientation sur l'éducation,* primary school teaching is divided into three multiyear cycles. The aim of these divisions is to cater to the different speeds at which individual pupils acquire knowledge. Its aim is also to limit the number of students repeating years.

Cycle 1 covers the first years in the école maternelle system up to age 5 (toute petite, petite, and moyenne sections). It is called *the early learning skills cycle (cycle des apprentissages premiers).*

Cycle 2 is called *the basic learning skills cycle,* involving three different levels: the upper level in école maternelle (grande section), the first year in elementary school (*cours préparatoire*), and the second year in elementary school (*cours élémentaire 1*) (see Figure 3.1). This second cycle bridges the last year of école maternelle (grande section) and the first 2 years of elementary school.

FIGURE **3.1. Multiyear Cycles Create a Bridge for Children**

	École maternelle: level 1
Cycle 1: The early learning skills cycle	
	École maternelle: level 2
	École maternelle: level 3
Cycle 2: The basic learning skills cycle	Elementary school: 1st grade
	Elementary school: 2nd grade

Cycle 3 is the further development of learning skills gathering the 3rd year (*cours élémentaire 2*), the 4th year (*cours moyen 1*), and the 5th year of elementary school (*cours moyen 2*).

In rural areas, classes are sometimes small (6 to 15 pupils). Pupils can be put together in one class, called "*classe unique*" (single class), in which pupils of the three different levels are taught together in one class by one teacher.

The aim of this chapter is to underline the particularities of French school attendance of children from 3 to 8. I will examine the historical context that favored the involvement of the French state in the education of young children, and then I will discuss how schools work today. Finally, I will underline the challenges that should be taken up by the French school system.

FROM SHELTERS TO THE ÉCOLE MATERNELLE

From the 18th century onward, working-class mothers were employed by the expanding industries in towns. Some factories allowed mothers to mind babies in the workshops. In this way mothers could take care of them. From the age of 2, many children were left on their own in the streets. Thus, older sisters minded some of them, or better-off parents paid a local child minder. However, often the child minders looked after children in slums, and many were illiterate.

The Creation of Shelters

Some parents sent their children to school when they reached the age of 4. However, schools were not adapted to such young children. Texts written in 1834 noted that young pupils were wasting their time at school and, at the same time, disturbing the schoolmaster. They became hostile to schooling: "their minds have been defeated by instruction beyond their understanding, by intimidation or by tedious immobility" (Cochin, 1834).

For those who were interested in early childhood, these places were considered to be harmful for children's development. There was a growing interest in childrearing at this time. Many people took initiatives to create educational systems for young children. Researchers had closely studied the history of early childhood institutions (Luc, 1997; Rollet, 1990). The invention of the young child was highlighted during this period, that is, the discovery of early stages of childhood with their own particular needs was recognized.

The first infant-minding center was created in the east of France by a minister named Oberlin (1740–1826). The "little knitting schools" (*petites écoles à tricoter*) took in young children. Their aim was to protect and care for children while their parents worked. Young children were taught the basics of moral and religious education, with knitting for girls and woodwork for boys. The British were positively influenced by this initiative. Under the impetus of Robert Owen (1777–1858), *infant schools* were created in England in 1817.

In France both Protestant and Catholic charitable institutions created establishments that specialized in assistance and childrearing. Their aim was to offer shelter and care for working-class children. They were the founders of the shelters, or *salles d'asile*.

The first shelter was created in 1826 by Emilie Mallet. This young mother, wife of a Protestant banker, had visited the infant schools. She was supported by the Christian Moral Society (*Société de la morale chrétienne*). This powerful philanthropic society with liberal tendencies considered this initiative a means of improving the life of the poor through care, work, and education.

Organization and Schedule of the Shelters

Jean-Denys Cochin (1789–1836) occupied a very important place among the patrons and philanthropists who supported the creation of the shelters (Luc, 1997). In 1833 he published the *Shelter Manual*. The influence of this book, intended as a guide for those in charge of shelters, is very important. This manual described the buildings, the layout, and the equipment. A shelter could care for about 100 children and offered a safe and healthy environment. In addition, their organization should be strict.

The architecture of a shelter consisted of an inside area and a covered playground. It was equipped with toilets, a fountain, and a porch. Children had their meals there. The classroom windows were placed 2 meters (about 6 feet) above ground level. In this way, children would not be disturbed by what was happening in the street.

The room was heated by a stove and was equipped with rows of seats with tables for writing. The mistress stood in the central aisle, which could also be used for gymnastics. Historical documents show the use of pedagogical material. There were blackboards and letter or number boards. There were also wall charts. The children used counting frames and small slates.

The curriculum was described in detail, such as how the care and schooling should be dispensed. Moral and religious education, physical exercises, reading, writing, and arithmetic were part of the timetable, along with geometry, sciences, geography, history, and even celestial physics. From 1850 onward, literacy became important. Legal texts written by the Ministry of Education, then called the Ministry of Instruction, defined the shelters as a preparation for the elementary school.

The Basis of Modern Education

In shelters, activities had to provide at the same time silence, order, and movement. Lessons alternated with "exercises in circles." During these exercises children were divided into several groups under the responsibility of "monitors." The monitors were the eldest children, who helped the mistress and her assistant.

There were several teaching methods used at this time. The "simultaneous method" perfected by the priests and nuns of church schools brought together about 30 pupils. The teaching was dispensed to the whole group. The exercises were chanted. This method was propagated 40 years later by the educational laws of Minister of Instruction Jules Ferry. The "mutual method" (helping one another) was widespread in England. The most advanced pupils acted as "monitors." From his rostrum the master gave orders to the monitors, seated at the end of the benches. In turn, they had to explain instructions to pupils in their row.

In the 1830s in France, the most widely used method for teaching schoolchildren in elementary schools was the "individual method." The master called the pupils one by one to teach them individually while the other pupils were left to their own devices.

Shelters were designed to take in many children. This explains the techniques of mass education with a necessity for strict discipline. The methods used in the shelters were based on repetition and immobility (children had to remain seated on the benches). This "well-tuned machine" marks "a new era in modern schooling, adapted to mass education." This organization "puts an end to the time wasting and disorder of individual teaching" (Dajez, 1994, p. 101).

From the 1830s onward, in industrial towns, two types of structure increased in number: a system of care for infants and shelters for older children. They were intended for children from working-class and poverty-stricken families. The aim of these structures was to free mothers from the worries of minding children and to promote their devotion to work. They also provided working-class offspring with better food and discipline from the very early years. Thanks to these care structures, children were protected from the physical and moral dangers of the streets.

At first, shelters were under hospital administration, but rapidly they were taken over by the Ministry of Instruction under the direction of the Minister Guizot. In fact, the Republicans were frightened that the Royalists and the Church would be too influential in the education of young children.

In 1833, the Guizot law marked the birth of public primary education. It ensured that each village had a school and each *département* (administrative region) had a schoolteacher training college (*école normale*). Shelters were defined as "houses of hospitality and education."

In 1837, an order clarified the "Shelter Charter." It specified that these were "charitable establishments." Children of both sexes could attend them up to a full 6 years, to receive maternal care and supervision and early education. Unpaid lady inspectors were assigned to supervise. They carried out their duties under university administration. A college was founded to train shelter mistresses.

TWO LEADING FIGURES OF THE ÉCOLE MATERNELLE

The first woman to leave her mark on the development of shelters was Marie-Pape Carpentier (1815–1878). The influence of the experiments of Friedrich Froebel (1782–1852), founder of the first kindergarten, is reflected in the importance attached to the respect for the child.

Head of a shelter, she was the author of about 40 books on education. In 1845 she published *Advice on the management of shelters* (*Conseils pour la direction des salles d'asile*). In 1848 she became the principal of a training college for head teachers and inspectors of shelters. The next year she became the principal of the mistresses' training college (*école normale*). The training lasted 3 months, and the school took in 1,500 students from all over Europe.

Marie-Pape Carpentier was the first woman lecturer at the Sorbonne in Paris. Under her influence, the term "shelter" was abandoned in favor of the term *école maternelle* in 1881. The law of 1881 (*Decree of 2 August 1881*) defined the école maternelle as the first level of primary school, not obligatory, and at no cost. Since that date, the organization of child care and education of children ages 2 through 6 has been responsibility of the French state.

Pauline Kergomard (1838–1925) was another woman who brought about important changes (Plaisance, 1996). This inspector of the Ministry of Education denounced the rigidity of shelter management. Influenced by the writings of 18th-century French philosopher Jean-Jacques Rousseau, she tried to defend an educational method founded on the respect for children. She contested the pressurized monotony imposed on children that, in fact, was like military training.

Pauline Kergomard took as an educational principle that the teaching of an école maternelle instructor should be the application of the educational methods of an attentive mother. She had noticed that normally, within a family, children develop physically and intellectually without taking lessons. This vision of spontaneity in child development replaced the strict model of the shelters.

Pauline Kergomard defended the idea that the école maternelle should not instruct but educate children. Repetitive techniques had to be abandoned for motor education and games. This is because play is the "profession of a child" (Kergomard, 1896). This choice showed another function of the école maternelle that was added to its care role: that of the protection of children with respect to their own specific needs (Chauveau & Rogovas-Chauveau, 1997).

Pauline Kergomard defended the recognition of a professional status for shelter mistresses. From 1887 onward, they could enter the teaching training colleges (*ecoles normales d'institutrices*). From then on, these training colleges trained teachers for both école maternelle and elementary school. As a result, one of the main difficulties of the école maternelle has been to break free from the influence of the elementary school model.

ÉCOLE MATERNELLE: A PLACE OF EDUCATION

Under the influence of Pauline Kergomard, things slowly began to change. The special needs of young children were acknowledged. Class numbers went down: They were limited to 50 pupils. Two sections were created: the small section (ages 2 to 5) and the older section (ages 5 to 7). Curriculum was influenced by the age of the children.

The identity of the école maternelle became apparent. The influence of specialized école maternelle inspectors was important. Research into infant psychology and the ideas of great educationalists were spread through a professional journal—*Infant Education*—founded in 1905.

The development of educational conferences allowed the creation of a training house for teachers. Work groups were formed in each region. Teachers discussed methods and reflected about their practices with pupils. In 1921, these groups amalgamated into an association of école maternelle teachers. An annual congress where researchers and teachers interacted promoted its national influence and contributed to an exchange of ideas. The association now exists under the name of AGEEM (General Association of École Maternelle Teachers). Its aims are to study educational issues and the defense and advancement of the rights and interests of children.

The work of Pauline Kergomard was sanctioned by the national curriculum law of 1921 (*Decree of 15 July 1921*). Children's activities were important in this école maternelle educational method. "Exercises" allowed children to develop their senses, their muscles, and their abilities. The curriculum listed timetable activities, in descending order of importance: "free games," mimed and sung sensorial and manual exercises, drawing and writing, language exercises, storytelling, observation exercises, and exercises concerning the rudiments of moral education.

This curriculum outlined a new model of socialization. A mission of collective education for young children is added to the original function of child care and protection (Chauveau & Rogovas-Chauveau, 1997). The age when children left school was raised to 14 in 1886. Therefore, the école maternelle had to prepare working-class pupils for a full education.

THE GENERALIZATION OF THE ÉCOLE MATERNELLE

Between the 1950s and the 1970s, the école maternelle evolved. Both social upheavals and the in-the-field work of teachers modified social expectations.

From the 1950s on, the école maternelle progressively became a place of education for all children aged 3 to 6 (Martin, 2002). The postwar population explosion, urbanization, and the increase in working mothers accounted for this important demand for schooling. Local authorities, responsible for the care of children since 1833, met this demand.

This was a time when many new schools were built. The buildings were more and more welcoming and functional. The furniture and the educational materials became more and more sophisticated, with greater variety.

The Ministry of National Education recruited large numbers of teachers. The situation was so urgent that they could not always be trained in the colleges (*écoles normales*). The inspectors, helped by educational advisers, ensured a training that was brief but nevertheless targeted toward the specific education of the école maternelle. Members of educational movements and of the AGEEM also invested a lot of energy in this work.

Local authorities are responsible for school transport and the upkeep and equipment of buildings. They hire the school helpers and the care staff who are in charge of before- and afterschool care centers. These are generally organized on the school premises, along with school catering. The financial contribution of families varies according to their earnings. Local authorities are also responsible for the école maternelle assistant (ATSEM). In the smallest section and small section, the école maternelle assistant supervises the afternoon nap and sometimes is also responsible for cleanliness. Under the responsibility of the teacher, she helps in taking care of the children and conducting activities, particularly since she has an early childhood degree (Bosse-Platière, 2007). When a disabled child is present in the class, a school assistant (AVS) is also needed.

Since 1959, schooling has been compulsory for all children aged 6 to 16. The new Education Law of 2005 has not made any modifications. In practice, children attend school long before the compulsory age. According to the Ministry of Education, since the 1970s, 100% of children from age 5 to 6 have attended the école maternelle (Ministry of Education [MEN], 2007a). Since 1980, 100% of children go to school at age 4. Since 1992, more than 95% of children go to school at age 3. Since 1981, about 35% of children aged 2 to 3 attend school (see Table 3.1). It is necessary to consider these figures with caution for two reasons. First, we do not have data concerning the schooling of Gypsies' children. Second, schools have had the obligation to accept children with disabilities since 2005 only. In 2006, the average length of schooling before age 6 was 3 years and 1 month. These figures include both state and private schools. However, state education takes up a large share because 85% of children attend a state school. In 2005, the average annual state expenditure per pupil was 4,660 euros for the école maternelle and 5,060 euros for elementary school (MEN, 2007a).

DEVELOPMENT AND DIVERSIFICATION OF TEACHING MODELS

The identity of the école maternelle became more apparent out of Ministry control and under the influence of advances in research on child psychology. Educational methods changed. The spread of the ideas of great educationalists such as Maria Montessori (1870–1952), Ovide Decroly (1871–1932), and Célestin Freinet (1896–1966) fostered new teaching methods (Francis, 2007).

After 1968, models of *"Education Nouvelle" (New Education)* spread due to the influence of the new education movements. Parents from more upper-class contexts wanted educational options that kept child development at the center of their concerns. The education offered by the école maternelle went beyond the one offered by the family. The reputation of this first school increased.

The recruitment of pupils was a sign of changing trends. From 1960 to 1970, 94% of the children of senior executives attended the école maternelle, compared to 80% of the children of unskilled workers and 58% of the children of farmers (MEN, 1973).

TABLE **3.1.** Percentage Enrollment in School for Children Age 2–6

Age (years)	1960 –1961	1970 –1971	1980 –1981	1990 –1991	2000 –2001
2–6	50	65.4	82.1	84.2	84.9
2–3	9.9	17.9	35.7	35.2	35.3
3–4	36	61.1	89	98.1	100
4–5	62.6	87.3	100	100	100
5–6	91.4	100	100	100	100

Source: Ministère de l'Education Nationale, 2004

During this period, two models of socialization influenced école maternelle teaching (Plaisance, 1986). After the war, the prevailing model of socialization was standardized and "productive." It met with the expectations of the working classes, who were attached to educational activities identified as useful as preparation for the "big school." From the 1970s on, the prevailing model of socialization was the "expressive" model. Activities of expression, particularly oral and artistic, developed the personality of each child. The development of this model is linked to the expectations of middle- and upper-class families. Sociological analysis shows that cultural similarity between these families and the teachers encouraged this trend (Chamboredon & Prévot, 1973).

In 1975, the national curriculum reflected this trend. The programs encouraged "free activities" and "free expression." It is emphasized that children can bloom only by acknowledging their classmates and teacher as fellow beings, free like them to act, imagine, and criticize. Education and development are the goals. It is never a question of training. Observing was recommended for two reasons: "detecting disabilities" and "defining goals according to the sociocultural background of each pupil."

Fifty-four years after the 1921 curriculum, the école maternelle was clearly defined for the first time as "a place of care and activities." The educational aspects are divided under six headings: emotional, corporal (movement, action, and self-expression), artistic expression, vocal expression and music, oral language and written language, and cognitive development.

The underlying idea of this model is that a rich environment encourages the learning abilities of children. The recommended methods became more natural. Exercises are abandoned in favor of "centers of interest." The principle is to amalgamate all the different sorts of school activities around a theme that is attractive for children. In order to encourage contact between children and between the child and the teacher, the class can be split up into small groups (*ateliers*). But studies show the detachment of the lower classes: The école maternelle began to seem irrelevant or unfamiliar (Chamboredon & Prévot, 1973; Plaisance, 1986). The activities and working methods offered, with an important place for contemporary arts and child expression, were nearer to the social models of middle- and upper-class families.

THE LINK BETWEEN
THE ÉCOLE MATERNELLE AND THE ELEMENTARY SCHOOL

From the 1980s on, academic failure and its causes began to be understood. Statistical assessments analyzed schooling. They showed the importance of preschool in the battle against poor performance in school.

From this point of view, the place of learning skills became apparent. In 1986 the national curriculum began with the following sentence: "The école maternelle is a school" (MEN, 1986). Its first goal is to provide schooling for children. It should give children the feeling that school is for learning. Learning has its own demands, satisfactions, and delights. Its second aim is to socialize in order to teach children how to establish relations with others and become sociable.

This new curriculum was welcomed by many teachers with relief and satisfaction. Its enforcement was made easier by the 1989 Educational Guidance Act (*Loi d'orientation sur l'école de 1989*). It established the primary school cycle system. The école maternelle found itself in a linking position between cycle 1–the early learning skills cycle–and cycle 2–the basic learning skills cycle.

Cycle 2 is the cycle of basic learning skills because it is within this cycle that pupils learn how to read and write. The upper-level class (*grande section*) is the last year of the école maternelle but is also part of cycle 2 (2nd level). It can be considered as a link between the école maternelle, "the little school," and elementary school, "the big school." This tends to encourage teamwork among the école maternelle and the elementary school teachers.

This transitional position aims to facilitate access to reading and writing for young children. Research has shown the importance of starting cultural activities with reading and writing as early as possible (Bonnafé, 1994; Corbenois, Devanne, & Dupuy, 2000; Hardy, Royon, & Breaute, 1996). This is to develop the child's interest for literacy and combat cultural exclusions. Structuring the progression of learning skills was expected to reduce the difficulties of adapting to the "big school."

Additional structures are in place to promote coherence across écoles maternelles and elementary schools. The Ministry of Education did away with the position of école maternelle inspector, instead giving all the inspectors responsibility for the assessment of écoles maternelles and elementary schools. These inspectors, located all over France, monitor teachers, who are assessed every 3 years. Teachers are recruited by the French state. Since 1991, they have been trained in the University Teacher Training Institutes (IUFM). There is no specialized training for teaching in the école maternelle or in the elementary school.

Since 1990, in each school every 4 years, the teaching staff and administrators develop a school project, *projet d'école,* that guides the educational activities. This project, of an artistic, scientific, or athletic kind, encourages teamwork. It brings together pupils and teachers of different classes of one cycle. Cultural, educational, or social participants, employed by the local authorities or social services, can take part in this project.

In 2002, the joint publication of the curricula of the three cycles of primary school underlined the need to continue to review and progress (MEN, 2002). These curricula describe with precision the subjects and the objectives that should be reached in each cycle. They specify how the 26 weekly hours of the timetable should be allocated for the cycles 2 and 3. Ten hours should be devoted to mastering the French language, with 2½ hours of reading and writing daily.

Early Schooling and Educational Success

In 1975, almost half the pupils entering secondary education had repeated a year. Today, the figure is two pupils out of ten (MEN, 2007a). This can be attributed to various factors, the first being the reduction in the size of classes. At the end of 1960, the average size of the école maternelle classes was 40 pupils. Today the average size is 30 pupils.

The second factor concerns the generalization of schooling for children aged 3 to 5. Early schooling is considered favorable to educational success. A study (Bernoussi, Florin, & Khomsi, 1994) compared the abilities of children who started school at age 2 with those of children who started at age 3. The results showed a better level of skills during the last 2 years of the école maternelle (at 4 and 5 years old) for children who started at age 2. This is most obvious in language skills, particularly for children from deprived backgrounds.

Other research (Jarousse, Mingat, & Richard, 1992), carried out on 4,000 children, shows that those who started school at age 2 have better results in French language and mathematics at the end of cycle 2 (8 years old). This advantage is identical whatever the social background. This positive effect wears out in the middle term. But in the long term, early schooling helps social integration for children from underprivileged families. Another study showed that the pupils who entered school at age 2 have a better level of skills at the entrance to the first elementary class, and this advantage continues for 2 more years (Caille, 2001).

Structuring Learning to Achieve Language Ability

Since the 1990s, an important place has been accorded to cultural awakening through music and the theatrical, visual, and fine arts, as well as the place given to books following experiments initiated by the ACCES association (Cultural Action Against Exclusion and Segregation).

But assessments carried out each year on young French people at age 17 show that nearly 11.7% of them have difficulties with reading comprehension and 4.8% are nearly illiterate (MEN, 2007b). The struggle against illiteracy is therefore one of the priorities. It is why the national curriculum already emphasized the fundamental role of the école maternelle in commanding oral, written, and visual languages. The curriculum published in 2002 structures children's learning around five domains of activities: These are oral language and an introduction to reading and writing; learning how to live together; expressing emotions and thoughts with one's body; discovering the world; and imagining, feeling, and creating. This curriculum places language at the heart of learning.

The curriculum includes a reference document of skills for each activity area and for each cycle. These reference documents were created by teachers and researchers in 2000–2001 for parents and educators. They can be purchased in any bookstore. For the école maternelle, exercises for children in the last year (*grande section*) are defined in the same five areas. The goal is to evaluate pupils at elementary school entry, and also to support their learning. Teachers and specialists can provide additional support in identified needs. During schooling, all these evaluations are marked in a notebook, *livret d'évaluation*.

The Department of Forecasts and Development (*Direction de la Prospective et du Développement*) devises assessments in French language and in mathematics. Since 1989, the abilities of all French pupils are assessed at the end of cycle 2 according to a national procedure. The results of these assessments are processed by a statistical program found on a national web site. Teachers can compare their pupils' results with national results, situate the achievements of the class as compared with other children, and identify the particular needs of their students. This system includes links to a data bank of teaching aids directly available in the class.

These curricula are regularly complemented by detailed supporting documentation. Devised by teachers, inspectors, and researchers, they are invaluable documents for teachers. They show examples of progression, learning sequences, situations of interaction between the teacher and pupils with learning difficulties, pupils' work, and so on.

CURRENT CHALLENGES TO IMPROVING THE SYSTEM

We can stress the fact that European research on comparative education recognizes that France has generous policies toward early education (Baudelot, 2002). School attendance for children aged 3 and older is free and widespread.[1] However, several aspects of education could be improved.

Adoption of Methods Adapted to the École Maternelle

The first point deals with the adult–children ratio. Whereas the ratio recommended by the early childhood system is 1:15 for children aged 3 to 6, the actual ratio is from 1:15 to 1:30 in the école maternelle in France (OECD, 2001). The second point concerns new curricula and methods. Each IUFM organizes continuing teacher training (usually 3 weeks) in order to help teachers adapt to these curricula, discover supporting documents, and examine their methods and practices. For the école maternelle, a great number of training courses deal with language development. This is an important challenge. For most of the pupils from working-class backgrounds, school is the first place where they become experienced in writing and reading papers.

In cycle 2, students' difficulties are linked with their limited access to cultural references and oral and written activities. The role of school is therefore to offer situations that are at the same time open and structured. These situations must be sufficiently open to arouse an interest in writing, to encourage the involvement of each pupil in authentic communication situations. They should be sufficiently structured to form a directory of cultural, linguistic, and cognitive references and to make this directory available.

One of the goals of schooling concerns the development of oral teaching, which is often difficult to apply. Results of research conducted by the psychologist Agnès Florin (1991, 1995) show, for example, that verbal communication in class is extremely centered around the teacher. She suggests themes for school conversation. Children often have a reactive role: They are invited to answer questions. Their interventions are brief. Verbal exchanges between pupils are not really encouraged. As the rules of school conversation are complex and often implicit, only the most competent children are likely to talk. This is why, in certain classes, up to 40% of children hardly talk or never talk during school conversations (Florin, 1991, 1995).

But as one of the great psychologists, Jerome Bruner (1983), has found, "we learn to speak by speaking." By interaction children construct their knowledge. The école maternelle curriculum considers children as active, reacting to their environment, involved in cultural learning, supported by the help of the teacher. The programs encourage a socioconstructivist approach.

Educational models of the école maternelle are close to project pedagogy. The project (for example, organizing a fruit-picking session in an orchard, taking part in musical meetings) gives rise to activities for a clearly defined amount of time. It gives a meaning to these activities for the children and it facilitates their involvement.

Three types of situation allow the implementation of the projects: cultural impregnation situations,[2] research situations,[3] and play and practice[4] (Baudelot, 2002; OECD, 2001). They can involve the whole class or be organized in small groups. The timetable, compulsory for each class, alternates the five activity areas and different means of organization. Teaching is often dynamic. It is backed up by the interest of children, by their trials and errors.

But real situations in classrooms show the use of several different methods. The cultural approach to learning can be replaced by regular learning of reading and writing. The use of ready-made exercise cards from cycle 1, the early learning skills cycle, is one of the dangers and can be seen in certain classes. In fact, a great number of school publishers sell books of exercises on writing, an introduction to reading, to mathematics, and so on. This supporting material is often used without discovery sessions and practical work. In this sort of situation, children work on their own and there is little interaction between them.

Some teachers meet with legal demands from the Ministry of Education by establishing strict progressions from the beginning of cycle 1. Activities leave little scope for exploration, discovery, or sensory experiments. In these classes there is a discernible reference to the traditional transmission model of teaching. Methods can show demands that are not adapted and difficulties in realizing the psycho-affective needs of young children and in respecting their own space. This could go against the first objective of the école maternelle: to allow for each child a successful first school experience.

The traditional three objectives of the école maternelle are care and assistance, awakening interests, and preparation for elementary school. This institution today is specifically tuned to the development of early skills. While this is to ensure easier transition between the école maternelle and the elementary levels, the risk of an overly rigid approach cannot be ignored, with learning situations thus set within a defined program, in particular for the youngest.

However, attending school from age 2 has been the subject of many debates. Since 1981, about 25% of children aged 2 to 3 go to school. By being part of the social structures, added to the fact that it is free of charge, école maternelle exerts an undeniable attraction for parents, including parents of 2-year-old children. Researchers (Florin, 2007; Rayna, 2004), inspectors of the ministry of education (Bouysse, 2007; Gioux, 2000), and some teachers and teacher educators seek to strengthen the quality of the school by attaching more importance to all the factors necessary for good cognitive, social, and emotional development of the children. To ensure a good-quality psycho-affective environment, groups should not exceed 20 children. Timetables should be flexible. Teaching should be exclusively centered on sensorial, motor, and cultural experiences.

This debate is healthy. It is approached as an occasion for the école maternelle to define an appropriate educational identity and to get its way among the institutions of the early childhood. This debate can also be the opportunity to define teacher training (Bouysse, 2007). The place given to child psychology and sociology of learning is too limited. The contents of training and its current organization—7 months of preparation for the competitive exam and 10 months of professional training—are insufficient for sound reflection on the particularities of école maternelle teaching.

Help for Children with Disabilities and Other Challenges

In France children of working parents and children with disabilities take priority in crèches and child care centers. A financial contribution, certainly small, is demanded of all families apart from deprived ones.

Children with mental, hearing, visual, or physical disabilities are in ordinary schools in special elementary classes: classes of school integration (CLIS). The objective is to offer them schooling adapted to their capacities and to the nature of their disability. A Network of Specialized Help for Pupils in Difficulty (RASED), composed of a school psychologist and specialized teachers, intervenes at the request of teachers or parents. A Specialized Aid Project is worked out after meeting the family. An assessment leads to psychological monitoring, in a state educational medical unit or in private medical structures. Educational support actions are organized by teachers who specialize in school re-education. Their aim is to help pupils, alone or in small groups, to ensure a better understanding of methods and work techniques, to become aware of their progression.

The RASED has a preventive mission. This is why they operate essentially with pupils in cycle 1 and 2 and in schools situated in Priority Education neighborhoods (*Zone d'Education Prioritaire* [ZEP]). In France, children attend the school that is in their place of residence, according to the school zone division in force. The mixing of pupils from different social backgrounds is not very common, especially in large towns. The ZEP neighborhoods were created in 1982. Their aim is to reinforce the educational act in all establishments where school populations are hit by poverty. In ZEP areas 52% of schoolchildren come from families where both parents are unemployed, against a national average of 8% (Davaillon & Nauze-Fichet, 2004). In each region, the Ministry of Education establishes the map of schools situated in ZEP areas from demographical data. Poverty and exclusion concern approximately 1 million children in France. It is necessary to understand and analyze better school and social trajectories to support these children and their families (Prêteur & de Léonardis, 2005).

In ZEPs, schools receive additional funds in order to reduce the child–staff ratios. There are bigger educational budgets and sometimes extra teacher and educational aids. This policy was reinforced in 2006 by the Projects of Educational Success (PRE). Set up in every municipality, the PRE has two objectives: to propose help targeted to children in trouble and to support the educational skills of their parents. Each PRE enters into an agreement of achievement to coordinate the action of the different educational partners: teachers, parents, special education teachers, social workers, and judicial workers. This contract, implemented for 3 years, is coordinated by a person in charge from the Ministry of Education and assessed by the regional department.

In order to create a good-quality educational network, a partnership is developed with local associations, sports and cultural structures, in particular with libraries. A *charter of educational support* encourages support plans for pupils from cycles 2 and 3 out of school hours. For example, for the pupils from the first year of elementary school, *cours préparatoire*, who are learning how to read, the experience of Help Clubs (*Clubs Coup de Pouce*) seems positive (Chauveau,

2000). Children are helped to learn how to read by retired people or students. Parents are invited to observe the help offered to their children. By following their progress, they better understand the action of the school. These meetings act as a basis for the development of new parental abilities.

The report by Moisan and Simon (1997) compares the functioning of more than 400 schools situated in ZEP areas. This report shows the existence of important qualitative differences. In "efficient ZEP schools" the results of pupils at the end of cycle 2 are at the same level as the national average or at less than 10% from this average. To be efficient, schooling depends on consistent educational choices. In these schools, more than 50% of pupils started school before age 3. Projects are centered on learning skills. They are actively guided by a coordinator. Collaboration between partners (teachers, parents, social workers, etc.) is important.

For deprived families, particularly immigrant families, the importance of schooling from the age of 2 or 3 is not always understood. Social services therefore try to facilitate attendance at care structures for young children. But school must also make progress to develop relations with parents, especially with migrant families, to facilitate children's schooling (Houchot, 1997). The weak recognition of the languages and cultures of the young children of migrant families can be an impediment to their success (Brougère, Guénif-Souilamas, & Rayna, 2007).

Ministerial texts insist on the necessity of coordinated childrearing practices between the school and the family. They give examples of encouraging experiences where the circulation of illustrated books between school and family (*cahiers de vie*) favors family verbal exchanges about the child's school experience. Research shows that these exchanges have several beneficial roles: They contribute to the development of children (Francis, 2000), they help the integration of parents, particularly mothers (Kohn, Abdat, Callu, & Famery, 1994), and they allow early parental involvement in the child's schooling (Francis, 2005). In order to help these exchanges, "relay ladies" or mediators, employed by certain local authorities, work in collaboration with parents and teachers from ZEP schools. This ecological perspective inspired by Bronfenbrenner (1979), who asserts the importance of integrating the complex system of the relations among parents, children, and professionals, inspires the policies on childhood in France (Doucet-Dahlgren, 2007).

Provision of Positive Education

Some experiences where the Ministry of Education and the municipalities are closely associated promote the quality of care and education (Dupraz, 1995; Lesur, 2007). Big towns currently enroll about 32% of their 2-year-olds in the école maternelle. Some develop certain requirements for welcoming them. These requirements concern their emotional comfort and materials organization—for example, having a specific relaxation and psychomotor activity room near the classroom.

In these cities, joint care experiences (nurseries, school, and the Department of Infant and Mother Protection, which provides child care for working mothers) are in operation. School timetables are adapted according to the children's age, while it is normal elsewhere to have an identical timetable for all children from cycle 1 to cycle 3 (6 hours a day, 5 days a week, during six 7-week cycles). In certain cases, a kindergarten teacher works with the école maternelle teacher and the école maternelle assistant. In other cases, children attend school in the morning and go to the nurseries or to a child minder in the afternoon. More personalized relations with families help the children to adapt. These methods are especially for schools situated in ZEP areas, where school attendance at 2 years old is encouraged. But financial restrictions prevent more development of these methods.

LOOKING FORWARD

A report by Eurostat (2005) indicates that in Europe, preschool centers are more and more frequented by young children. Furthermore, the distinction between school and preschool models has been reduced. In France, care structures for children have already existed for a long time. But improvement is needed in developing the quality of early schooling. Three points could be improved: First, a better balance should be found between being a child and being a schoolchild. Second, in schools, parents should be fully recognized as partners. It seems that on these two first points, legal texts are ahead of most school practices. School practices and legal texts seem to come together on a third point: There is a need to develop attention to children with special needs, whether it is children with disabilities or underprivileged children.

NOTES

1. École maternelle for 2-year-olds is also free, when available, but is not as widespread.

2. In these situations pupils meet with literary, artistic, and technological forms. They discover how to identify and create (sculptures, poems, stories).

3. These productive situations can be guided or directed by the teacher and give rise to a reflexive approach. Children are invited to venture hypotheses, to use them, and to compare them.

4. These situations are to develop particular skills in the areas of language, mathematical logic, motor, graphical, and linguistic skills.

REFERENCES

Baudelot, O. (2002). *Accueil et éducation des jeunes enfants en Europe* [Early childhood education and care in Europe]. Paris: Actes du séminaire.

Bernoussi, M., Florin, A., & Khomsi, A. (1994). *La scolarisation des enfants de deux ans: Apprentissages fondamentaux et scolarisation à deux ans: Analyse rétrospective* [Schooling two-year olds: Basic learning and schooling at two years of age: Retrospective analysis]. Rapport à la Direction des Écoles [Report for the Department of Schools]. Nantes: Université de Nantes, Laboratoire de psychologie–Labécd.

Bonnafé, M. (1994). *Les Livres c'est bon pour les bébés* [Books are good for babies]. Paris: Calmann-Lévy.

Bosse-Platière, S. (2007). La place de l'ATSEM dans l'équipe éducative à l'école maternelle [The place of the école maternelle specialized territorial agent in the école maternelle educational team]. In N. Geneix & L. Chartier (Eds.), *Petite Enfance: Enjeux éducatifs de 0 à 6 ans* [Early childhood: Educational stakes from 0 to 6 years of age] (pp. 77–82). Paris: Observatoire de l'enfance en France/ESF.

Bouysse, V. (2007). L'école maternelle française: de l'assurance au doute [The French école maternelle: From confidence to doubt]. In N. Geneix & L. Chartier (Eds.), *Petite Enfance: Enjeux éducatifs de 0 à 6 ans* [Early childhood: Educational stakes from 0 to 6 years of age] (pp. 109–115). Paris: Observatoire de l'enfance en France/ESF.

Bronfenbrenner, U. (1979). *The ecology of human development: Experiments by nature and design.* Cambridge, MA: Harvard University Press.

Brougère, G., Guénif-Souilamas, N., & Rayna, S. (2007). De l'usage de l'altérité pour comprendre le préscolaire [Using alterity to understand preschool]. In G. Brougère & M. Vandenbroeck (Eds.), *Repenser l'éducation des jeunes enfants* [Rethinking early childhood education] (pp. 263–288). Brussells: PIE Peter Lang.

Bruner, J. (1983). *Child's talk, learning to use language* (French edition: *Comment les enfants apprennent à parler*). New York: W.W. Norton.

Caille, J.-P. (2001). Scolarisation à 2 ans et réussite de la carrière scolaire au début de l'école élémentaire [Schooling at 2 years of age and success in school trajectory at the beginning of elementary school]. *Education & Formations* [Education and Training], *2001*(60), 7–18. MEN/Ministère de l'Education Nationale de l'enseignement supérieur et de la recherche.

Chamboredon, J.-C., & Prévot, J. (1973). Le Métier d'enfant. Définition sociale de la prime enfance et fonctions différentielles de l'école maternelle [The job of being a child. Social definition of early childhood and differential functions in the école maternelle]. *Revue Française de Sociologie* [French Sociology Review], *14*, 295–335.

Chauveau, G. (2000). *Comment réussir en ZEP* [How to succeed in the Priority Education Zone]. Paris: Retz.

Chauveau, G., & Rogovas-Chauveau, E. (1997). L'Ecole maternelle et les milieux populaires [The école maternelle and working-class sectors]. *Migrants-Formation* [Migrants Training], *110*, 83–95.

Cochin, J.-D. (1834). *Manuel des salles d'asile*, 2ème édition [*Salles d'Asile* manual, 2nd edition]. Paris: Hachette.

Corbenois, M., Devanne, B., & Dupuy, E. (2000). *L'Album source d'apprentissages, apprentissages de la langue et conduites culturelles à l'école maternelle* [The album as a learning source: Learning language and cultural behavior at the école maternelle]. Paris: Bordas.

Dajez, F. (1994). *Les Origines de l'école maternelle* [The origins of the école maternelle]. Paris: Presses universitaires de France.

Davaillon, A., & Nauze-Fichet, E. (2004). Les trajectoires scolaires de enfants pauvres [School trajectories of low income children]. *Education & Formations* [Education and Training], *2003-2004, 70*. MEN/Ministère de l'Education Nationale de l'enseignement supérieur et de la recherche. Retrieved from http://media.education. gouv.fr/file/12/9/5129.pdf

Doucet-Dahlgren, A-M. (2007). Quelles évolutions des modes d'accueil des jeunes enfants en France [Evolution of types of early childcare in France]. In D. Fablet (Ed.), *L'Education des jeunes enfants: Pour de nouvelles modalités d'accueil éducatif* [Early childhood education: New educational child care modes] (pp. 61–78). Paris: L'Harmattan.

Dupraz, L. (1995). *Le Temps d'apprivoiser l'école: Lieux et actions-passerelles entre les familles et l'école maternelle* [Time to tame the school: Places and linking actions between families and the école maternelle]. Paris: Ed. Fondation de France.

Eurostat. (2005). *Les chiffres clés de l'éducation en Europe 2005 (6e édition)* [Key facts in European education, 6th edition]. Office des publications officielles des Communautés européennes (EUR-OP). Retrieved from http://www.eurydice.org/ressources/ eurydice/pdf/0_integral/052EN.pdf

Florin, A. (1991). *Pratiques du langage à l'école maternelle et prédictions de la réussite scolaire* [Language practice at the école maternelle and school success predictions]. Paris: Presses universitaires de France.

Florin, A. (1995). *Parler ensemble en maternelle: La maîtrise de l'oral, l'initiation à l'écrit* [Talking in the école maternelle: The mastery of speech, the beginning of writing]. Paris: Éditions Marketing.

Florin, A. (2007). Les différents modes d'accueil et leurs effets sur les jeunes enfants. In N. Geneix & L. Chartier (Eds.), *Petite enfance: Enjeux éducatifs de 0 à 6 ans* [Early childhood: Educational stakes from 0 to 6 years of age] (pp. 61–68). Paris: Observatoire de l'enfance en France/ESF.

Francis, V. (2000). Les Mères des milieux populaires face à l'école maternelle. Accès à l'information et rapport à l'institution [Working-class mothers facing the école maternelle. Information access and rapport with the institution]. *Les Sciences de L'éducation pour L'ère Nouvelle, Revue Internationale* [Education Sciences for the New Age, International Review], *33*(4), 83–108.

Francis, V. (2005). Le partenariat école/famille: Le rôle de l'enfant messager [School/ family partnership: The role of the messenger child]. In S. Rayna & G. Brougère (Eds), *Accueillir et éduquer la petite enfance: Les Relations entre parents et professionnels* [Childhood education and care: Parent/professional provider relationships] (pp. 41–70). Paris: INRP.

Francis, V. (2007). Early childhood education pedagogy in France. In M. Cochran & B. New (Eds.), *Early childhood education: An international encyclopedia* (pp. 1076–1080). Westport, CT: Praeger.

Gioux, A.-M. (2000). *Première école, premiers enjeux* [First school, first stakes]. Paris: Hachette.

Hardy, M., Royon, C., & Breaute, M. (1996). Pédagogie interactive et premiers apprentissages [Interactive teaching and early learning]. In S. Rayna, F. Laevers, & M. Deleau (Eds.), *L'Education préscolaire: Quels objectifs pédagogiques?* [Preschool education: What pedagogical objectives?] (pp. 255–274). Paris: INRP/Nathan.

Houchot, A. (1997). L'Ecole maternelle et les enfants d'immigrés: L'école de la réussite pour tous? [The école maternelle and immigrant children: Success school for all?]. *Migrants-Formation* [Migrant Training], *110*, 101–115.

Jarousse, J.-P., Mingat, A., & Richard, C. (1992). La scolarisation maternelle à 2 ans: Effets pédagogiques et sociaux [École maternelle schooling at 2 years of age: Pedagogical and social effects]. *Education et Formation* [Education and Training], *31*, 3–9. MEN/ Direction de l'Evaluation et de la Prospective.

Kergomard, P. (1896). *L'Education maternelle dans l'école* [École maternelle education in the school]. Paris: Hachette.

Kohn, R., Abdat, O., Callu, E., & Famery, K. (1994). Les Initiatives parentales: La dynamique de leur articulation avec les initiatives instituées pour l'éducation des enfants [Parent initiatives: The dynamics of their articulation with the initiatives instituted for childhood education]. In J.-P. Pourtois & P. Durning (Eds.), *Éducation et famille* [Education and family] (pp. 163–188). Brussels: De Boeck Université.

Lesur, E. (2007). Les classes passerelles: Un espace éducatif entre école et famille [Linking classes: An educational space between school and family]. In D. Fablet (Ed.), *L'Education des jeunes enfants: Pour de nouvelles modalités d'accueil éducatif* [Early childhood education: New educational child care modes](pp. 156–174). Paris: L'Harmattan.

Luc, J.-N. (1997). *L'Invention du jeune enfant au XIXe siècle: De la salle d'asile à l'école maternelle* [The invention of childhood in the 19th century: From the salle d'asile to the école maternelle]. Paris: Editions Belin.

Martin, C. (2002, October). *L'accueil des jeunes enfants en Europe: Quelles leçons pour le cas français?* Rapport réalisé à la demande du Haut conseil à la population et à la famille [Childcare in Europe: Lessons for the French case. Report requested by the High Council for Population and Family].

MEN/Ministère de l'Education Nationale. (1973). *Études et documents* [Studies and documents], 28. Paris: CNDP.

MEN/Ministère de l'Education Nationale de l'enseignement supérieur et de la recherche. (1986). *Programmes pour l'école maternelle* [Programs for the école maternelle]. Paris: CNDP.

MEN/Ministère de l'Education Nationale de l'enseignement supérieur et de la recherche. (2002). *Qu'apprend-on à l'école maternelle?* [What do we learn in the école maternelle?]. Paris: CNDP.

MEN/Ministère de l'Education Nationale de l'enseignement supérieur et de la recherche. (2004). Les trajectoires scolaires des enfants pauvres [School trajectories of low income children]. *Education & Formations* [Education & Training], *70*. Retrieved from http://media.education.gouv.fr/file/12/9/5129.pdf

MEN/Ministère de l'Education Nationale de l'enseignement supérieur et de la recherche. (2007a). *L'Education nationale en chiffres, 2006–2007, Direction de l'evaluation, de la prospective et de la performance* [National education facts, 2006–2007, Department of Evaluation, Prospective and Performance]. Retrieved from http://media.education. gouv.fr/file/97/8/6978.pdf

MEN/Ministère de l'Education Nationale de l'enseignement supérieur et de la recherche. (2007b). Les compétences en lecture des jeunes [Child reading skills]. *L'Etat de l'École* [The State of the School], *17*. Retrieved from http://media.education.gouv. fr/file/05/3/7053.pdf

Moisan, C., & Simon, J. (1997). *Les Déterminants de la réussite scolaire en Zone d'Éducation Prior-*

itaire [Determinants of school success in the Priority Education Zone]. Paris: Ministère de l'éducation nationale, de l'enseignement supérieur et de la recherche/La Documentation Française.

OECD. (2001). *Starting strong: Early childhood education and care.* Paris: Author.

Plaisance, E. (1986). *L'Enfant, la maternelle, la société* [Child, école maternelle, and society]. Paris: Presses universitaires de France.

Plaisance, E. (1996). *Pauline Kergomard et l'école maternelle* [Pauline Kergomard and the école maternelle]. Paris: Presses universitaires de France.

Prêteur, Y., & de Léonardis, M. (2005). Précarités et scolarités [Insecurities and schooling]. *Empan,* 60–2005/4, 101–107.

Rayna, S. (2004). Some problems on école maternelle and crèches in France. In M. Takeuchi, S. Mori, & R. Scoot (Eds.), *New Directions in early childhood education in the 21st century: International perspectives* (pp. 161–183). Waverly, IA: G&R Publishing.

Rollet, C. (1990). La Politique à l'égard de la petite enfance sous la Troisième République [The politics of early childhood under the third republic]. *Cahier, 127.* Paris: Presses universitaires de France/INED.

CHAPTER 4

The German Educational System for Children from 3 to 10 Years Old

HANS-GUENTHER ROSSBACH

The following chapter consists of two parts. In the first part, the historical development of the German educational system for children from 3 to about 10 years old is outlined. Special emphasis is put on the relationship between pre-school education and compulsory school education. In the second part, selected current reform efforts, which seem to be of most importance for the further development of the German system, are presented.

THE HISTORICAL DEVELOPMENT OF THE EDUCATIONAL SYSTEM

Development of Compulsory School and the School Entrance Age

To understand the current shape of the educational system for young children in Germany, we have to go back about 400 years (Mader, 1989; Ruediger, Kormann, & Peez, 1976). In some regions of the Holy Roman Empire of the German Nation, general compulsory education was introduced in the 17th century. The reasons were mainly related to religious and economic interests for which illiteracy was dysfunctional. For example, general compulsory schooling was proclaimed in Weimar in 1619. However, the proclamation of general schooling was not equivalent with the realization of general school attendance. For a long period, only a small portion of the population attended schools. Especially for children of poor people and from the rural population, regular school attendance was impossible, since the working power of young children was urgently needed for the survival of families. In Prussia, for example, a regulation of 1763 provided that public herdsmen should be employed in order to allow the children to keep attending school during harvesttime. Not until the mid-19th century was general compulsory schooling established. However, there was not one school for all children, but different types of schools for children from different parts of the population. In Prussia, for example, there existed—among others—special schools for children from the aristocracy and from the bourgeoisie, for Catholic and for Evangelical children, schools for boys only and for girls only, army schools for children of officers, schools for poor children, schools for children of prisoners, and private preparatory schools for higher secondary schools. The most important step in the shaping of the current school system was taken in the Weimar Republic after World War I when, with the 1920 *Grundschulgesetz* (Elementary School Law), general compulsory schooling in one school for all children was enacted. Since that time, one school for all children covers the first four grades of compulsory schooling, before children are distributed to different types of schools at age 10 according to their level of achievement. The restriction of the one school for all children to only the first four grades of compulsory schooling was a compromise that was gained by fighting against conservatives and especially the advocates of the German *Gymnasium* (a rigorous 9-year secondary school).

During the period of the development of compulsory schooling, different ages were considered for the first year of school. In some regions, it was laid down that children should start compulsory school at the age of 5, in others at the age of 6 or even 7. Since the beginning of the 19th century, there has been a tendency to establish school entrance at age 6. In 1927 the *Schulpflichtgesetz* (Law on School Attendance), the entrance age was fixed at, on average, 6 years and 3 months (Herff, 1967). In the 20th century, the school entry age was slightly increased (from, on average, 6 years and 3 months to 6 years and 7 or 8 months). The latest agreement between the 16 Federal States of Germany was reached in 1997 (Rossbach, 2001). Compulsory schooling begins after the summer holidays (depending on the state, between July and September) for children who turn 6 by a set date. This date is set by each state and should be within the period from June 30 to September 30. Most states opted for June 30.

In all times, calendar age has not been the only criteria for sending children to school. Comenius, for example, argued in 1628 for a school start at age 6. However, the school start could be advanced or delayed for half a year or for a full year depending on the readiness and the achievement level of a child (Rue-diger, Kormann, & Peez, 1976). The same provision was included in the agreement of the 16 states in 1997 (Rossbach, 2001). Depending on readiness and achievement level, children could be admitted to school even if they turn 6 later in the year, up to December 31 (in special cases even if they turn 6 later than December 31). Children who have reached the age for starting school could be delayed for 1 year if it is assumed that their readiness and achievement level prevent adequate stimulation in compulsory school. In 2006, 7.1% of the children started compulsory school 1 year earlier than expected according to their age, and for 4.8% the school start was delayed for 1 year (in both cases, there exist significant differences between the German states; Autorengruppe Bildungsberichterstattung, 2008). Thus, we have two criteria for school start—calendar age and readiness/achievement level—which were differently emphasized at different times in the past. Currently, the political and educational discussion puts more emphasis on the criteria of calendar age. A delay of school start because of lack of readiness should be prevented or at least reduced. On the other side, early admission to compulsory school is supported.

In Germany, compulsory school (at all levels of general education) is provided free by the states because school education is considered a general value for which the government is responsible. In all states, the ministry of education is responsible for all areas of compulsory school. In general, school education is provided in public buildings and is financed by two sources: Construction and maintenance of the buildings is financed by the community (and sometimes at the state level, too), whereas the teachers are paid directly by the states. For private schools, which are very rare in Germany, other rules exist, which necessitate high parental fees.

Development of Preschool Education

The origins of the development of early childhood care and education must be seen against the background of the formation of the bourgeois notion of the family, which came into being during the second half of the 18th century (Rossbach, 2003; Tietze, Rossbach, & Ufermann, 1989). Accordingly, woman "discovered" within the family her "natural" vocation as wife and mother. However, members of a large number of social strata lacked the material means necessary to attain such a bourgeois family ideal. Because of the poverty of the lower classes, all capable family members, mothers as well as older children, were obliged to work. Many young children were left on their own, and accidents among children were common. As a consequence, various local establishments for the care and education of young children came into being. In most cases, their founding was initiated by members of the bourgeois class and the aristocracy. In the first half of the 19th century, the churches established infant schools for young children (*kleinkinderschulen,* infant schools, and *kleinkinderbewahranstalten,* infant care institutes). These foundations formed a starting point from which, during the second half of the 19th century, the Protestant and Roman Catholic churches gained decisive influence on early childhood education and care in Germany. The main goal of the kleinkinderschulen and kleinkinderbewahranstalten—which were open all day—was care of poor children in order to enable mothers' employment. In addition, the small children were to be educated according to bourgeois principles in order to instill in them morals appropriate to the circumstances of their class (ethics of the proletarian).

A different model was established by Friedrich Froebel (1782–1852) with his *Kindergarten.* Froebel emphasized educational goals oriented to support the development of children. Kindergartens were generally open for only a few hours a day and attended largely by middle-class children. A continual increase in the number of preschool institutions characterizes developments in the second half of the 19th century. Attempts were made to incorporate the pedagogical methods of the Froebel Kindergarten into the conceptual framework of institutions with largely welfare character. This resulted in the establishment of the *volkskindergarten* (people's Kindergarten). Since about the turn of the 20th century, child-oriented motives have been advanced as a justification for center-based preschool education. This was accompanied by a change in the age distribution because, in most preschools, the entrance age had now been raised to 3. Before, all children of preschool age could be found in the preschools (except—for more practical reasons—infants). Now, the younger children were assigned to crèches (*krippen*), which focused on care and had no educational justifications.

In the Weimar Republic after World War I, attempts were made to include Kindergarten in the educational system and to make it the foundation of a uniform educational system for all children. However, these attempts failed. The regulations laid down in the 1922 *Reichsjugendwohlfahrtsgesetz* (Youth Welfare Act) are even today still valid in principle. The law acknowledged the right of every child to an education, which the public authorities were obliged to provide indirectly or directly if the family itself was unable to do so. The law gave priority in the foundation and running of Kindergartens to organizing bodies of independent social welfare organizations (principle of subsidiarity). This means that Kindergartens sponsored by public authorities were only established if the need for such institutions was not met by the churches or other philanthropic organizations. With the Youth Welfare Act, the system of early childhood care and education in Germany has found its basic shape, which is—in the main features—still valid today. After World War II, the structures of the early childhood systems of the Weimar Republic were reinstated in West Germany (Federal Republic of Germany—FGR). In the German Democratic Republic (GDR—East Germany), different developments took place. After unification of the two German parts in 1990, however, a process began in which the structures of the former GDR were replaced by those from the FRG. Thus, the structure established in the Republic of Weimar lasted for more than 80 years and the social welfare organization (together with most of people in the early childhood field) put much emphasis on the preservation of this structure.

Kindergarten[1]—even if it is considered the elementary level of the general system of education—does not belong to the school system. It is part of the field of youth and social welfare and thus lies within the jurisdiction of the youth welfare law. The federal government possesses little jurisdiction in this field. Its tasks largely consist of enacting a frame law (*Kinder- und Jugendhilfegesetz*, Law on Child and Youth Welfare) and of formulating proposals, distributing information, and developing model projects. The establishment and operation of Kindergartens and other forms of nonfamilial early care and education (for younger children and for afterschool care) is regulated by acts put forth at the state level, which represents the implementation of the federal youth welfare enactment. The states enact special laws that mainly deal with general goals, the framework of finance, supply planning, equipment, participation of parents, responsibilities, and so forth. According to the principle of subsidiarity, independent organizations (such as churches, welfare, or other philanthropic organizations) operate most of the Kindergartens. In 2007, almost two-thirds of all places for children from birth up to school start were operated by independent organizations, the other places by public authority (Autorengruppe Bildungsberichterstattung, 2008). The agencies—independent organizations as well as public authorities like the communities—act for the most part autonomously, determining their own educational philosophies and goals. Furthermore, they provide for the operation of the institution, employ its personnel, supervise its operation, and are responsible for pedagogical advice and inservice training of personnel. They also provide the buildings, which are not connected to the buildings for compulsory schooling. Even if the field of early childhood care and education belongs to the field of youth and social welfare, Kindergartens are overseen in about half of the 16 states by the ministry of education and in the others by the ministry of youth and social welfare. In several of the states, there has been a shift from the ministry of youth and social welfare to the ministry of education in recent years, which is at least partly connected to the discussion to put more emphasis on cognitive stimulation and school preparation in Kindergarten.

Financing for the operation of institutions for early childhood care and education comes from four sources: the respective agency (e.g., welfare organization or community), community subsidies, state subsidies, and parental contributions. If the institution is operated by the community, the community has to cover the part of the agency, too (OECD, 2004). The federal level is not involved in the financing. The proportion from the four sources varies considerably from state to state. On average across all states, the states and the communities cover 75% to 80% of the costs, the parents around 14%, and the rest covered by the operating agencies. Parental contributions are set individually according to income and are further reduced in cases in which two or more children of the same family attend the same setting. Thus, contrary to compulsory schooling, which is free for all children, the parents have to pay a significant fee for care and education before the start of compulsory schooling.

Since 1996, the federal law on child and youth welfare has established a legal claim for a place in a Kindergarten for all children from age 3 up to the start of compulsory education. In 2007, 79.5% of all children aged 3 to 4, 92.5% of all children aged 4 to 5, and 94.8% of all children aged 5 to 6 attended Kindergarten (Autorengruppe Bildungsberichterstattung, 2008). In general, there are mixed-age groups in the German Kindergarten comprising three or even more age groups.

The Relation Between Preschool and Compulsory School

The relationship between preschool and compulsory schooling and the transition from one to the other are subjects of long-term debate among the public as well as in professional educational circles in Germany. For long parts of the history, this relationship can be characterized by dissociation and demarcation. Six overlapping periods in the history of the relationship between preschool and compulsory school can be distinguished (Rossbach & Erning, in preparation):

1. At the beginning of preschool education (about 1800 to 1830), younger children below the age of compulsory schooling were barred from elementary school. Unlike earlier, these smaller children were not admitted to school anymore in order to keep lessons disciplined and free of interruptions. Several school regulations in different parts of Germany barred children younger than age 5 from attending school. Excluding younger children from school created a need for a different type of institution, resulting in the kleinkinderschulen (infant schools) around 1826.

2. Regarding these kleinkinderschulen, the most prominent feature of the phase between 1826 and 1920 is the strict separation between and coexistence of infant school and elementary school. Infant schools were limited to the care of children from poorer families and there was no connection between the infant schools and the compulsory schooling system. On the contrary, when Bavaria, for example, installed general regulations in 1839, which can be viewed to be the first set of laws concerning child care in Bavaria, they banned all school-like content—reading, writing, and arithmetic—from the infant schools. Correspondingly, they prohibited the title "teacher" for all child care staff and the name "infant school." Instead they were now to be called *kleinkinderbewahranstalten* (which translates approximately to "small children keeping institutions"). Continuous play was recommended as the main stimulating entertainment.

3. While kleinkinderschulen and kleinkinderbewahranstalten were strictly separated from elementary schools, Froebel established with his Kindergarten a connection between them. For Froebel, the Kindergarten was the missing foundation for school. Froebel was not the defender of a thesis of straight separation between Kindergarten and elementary school, which he is sometimes—even today—viewed to have been. His emphasis was not set on two contrary systems. He rather focused on the didactic nature of school at that time, which led him to point out the educational tasks of early education before school. His position is not contrary to a coordination of educational

tasks in Kindergarten and elementary school. The perceived gap between "play" in Kindergarten and "lessons" in school is smaller than commonly assumed, as Froebel himself mentions "play as incidental lesson." As far as the method—play—is concerned, in his view Kindergarten is independent from the schooling system. Yet education in Kindergarten is always oriented toward human development, as it is continued in school. Froebel differentiates between Kindergarten age and school age in terms of "prerational presentiment" and "rational knowledge," which are different, but chronologically succeeding, cognition stages of preschool and school-age children.

4. The separation between the two educational levels of Kindergarten and elementary school was strengthened by the 1920 *Reichsschulkonferenz* (School Law). Any state influence on the Kindergarten curriculum was forbidden. Kindergarten was an object of welfare, with no connection to school. This separation of Kindergarten and school has lasted since then and was a characteristic of the West German system.

5. The developments in the former German Democratic Republic (GDR) were different. Between 1949 and 1989, Kindergarten was one level within the educational system and thus aimed at adequate school readiness for all children. Government officials designed and controlled the curriculum and all educational goals.

6. There are indications of a new phase starting in the 1990s, as today Kindergarten and school—both in need of reform—seem to carefully approach each other. The current proposal for reform emphasizes the bidirectional orientation of these two educational levels.

A better fit between Kindergarten and school is very often discussed from the perspective of different requirements and a great degree of discontinuity between the two levels, demanding more continuity. However, it is equally as erroneous to state that discontinuity in the requirements of the two settings is obstructive to learning efforts or general development as it is to presume that they provoke development and learning with certainty. The extent to which a lack of fit between the two educational settings in fact hinders children in their cumulative learning processes is an empirical question, which is by no means sufficiently answered yet.

Problems rising at the crossover of separated educational institutions can possibly be solved by assimilating or integrating the two (Faust & Rossbach, 2004). An example is the Dutch *Basisschule* (basic school), which comprises eight grades for 4- to 12-year-old students. The former Dutch Kindergarten was integrated with the 1st and 2nd grade of elementary school in 1985. Increased professional training for preschool teachers went parallel to these structural reforms. Today all education personnel for basic schools are trained equally intensively at the same institutes. Another example of unification of preschool and school can be seen in the German-speaking cantons in Switzerland, where projects are run that enroll 4-year-olds for 3 or 4 years in a basic level. This new educational institution combines 2 years of preschool with the first two grades, or at least with the 1st grade of elementary school. Classes contain mixed-age groups in which the children may stay for a different number of years according to their development. Such far-reaching reforms that interlock preschool and elementary school in one new institution are currently not planned in Germany. There are, however, several reform efforts discussed that would change certain aspects at the intersection of Kindergarten and elementary school.

CURRENT REFORM EFFORTS IN GERMANY

Different reform efforts with different ranges are discussed. There is no claim to cover all current German reform efforts completely. Rather, some are selected that are considered to be of most importance for further developments.

Decreasing School Entrance Age

At least to some degree, the official age for school start is arbitrary. There exists no "true" age for school start because the required achievement level of the children is dependent on the demands of the school system. Lowering or raising the demands of the school system will change the required achievement level, which, in turn, will influence the age considered necessary for school start.

Without changing the demands of the school system, several German states currently are lowering the school entrance age. This is part of general considerations to lower school leaving age. As has been described, compulsory schooling begins in Germany after summer holidays (depending on the state, between July and September) for children who turn 6 by a set date, which in most states is June 30. Currently, several of the 16 German states are planning or have already decided to shift this date nearer to the end of the year in order to decrease the school entrance age. In addition, many states encourage earlier admission to school, given a certain readiness and achievement level of a child.

Even if this lowering of the average age of school start is currently moderate, adjustment of the didactics and methods in 1st grade seems necessary, especially given that further decreases of the school entrance age are planned. In addition, it can be expected that, together with a certain oversupply of available places in Kindergartens because of the decline of the birth rate, children younger than age 3 (the current "official" age of start of Kindergarten) will be admitted to Kindergarten, which, in turn, will also demand certain adaptations in the pedagogy of Kindergarten.

Development of State Curricula for Early Childhood Education

As already mentioned, the federal government possesses little jurisdiction in the field of early childhood education. It only enacts a frame law (*Kinder-und Jugendhilfegesetz*, Law on Child and Youth Welfare) that is interpreted and supplemented by state laws. Even if the state laws deal with general goals, the operating agencies—independent organizations as well as public authorities like the communities—act, for the most part, autonomously. They decide on their own educational philosophies, goals, and methods. Thus, there has been little obligation in the educational work in the past.

Over the past few years, a new development can be seen in Germany. All states have developed or are developing educational plans for the early childhood care and education field, especially for Kindergarten[2] (Diskowski, 2005). These educational plans can be—at least partly—considered state curricula. Across the German states, there are similarities as well as differences. Differences, for example, exist in the extent of the plans, which range from less than 20 pages in one state to more than 400 pages in another state. Another difference refers to the age span for which these educational plans are developed. In some states, only children of the classical Kindergarten age (age 3 to entry into compulsory schooling) are referred to; in others, the age span from birth up to entry into compulsory schooling or even up to age 14 is covered. However, great similarities exist in that no educational plan formulates child outcome standards, which are strongly rejected. All educational plans cover comparable content areas in which the development of the children should be stimulated. These content areas are broadly conceptualized and should not be—as is stated in the plans—considered subjects the way they are in compulsory school. A high value is set on this demarcation from school subjects. On the other side, clear lines can be drawn from these content areas to the school subjects in elementary school, especially in educational plans that try to cover both Kindergarten and elementary school. Another similarity is that the educational plans address the transition process from Kindergarten to elementary school and offer coping strategies for children and their families.

The educational plans set expectations for the work in the Kindergartens. On the other side, they also emphasize that the educational plans have to be interpreted according to the special situation of a local Kindergarten and that they allow for freedom in the realization. In general, the expectations are met by consensus or contract with the umbrella organizations of the sponsoring agencies, and the umbrella organizations use their influence on their members (the local sponsoring agencies) with regard to an appropriate realization of the educational plans. However, such agreements do not really guarantee an appropriate realization of the plans because of the autonomy of the local sponsoring agencies in deciding on their educational philosophies, goals, and methods. The idea of enforcing these expectations by law is considered controversial, given the actual federal Law on Child and Youth Welfare, with the emphasis on parental rights to decide on the direction of the education of their children outside of compulsory schooling. Another possibility would be to approach the obligation by giving public financial support only to those Kindergartens that follow the respective educational plan. In such a case, it has to be shown that the educational plans are strictly based on current knowledge, that they are not following a specific educational orientation, and that their realization can be objectively checked—which does not seem to be realizable given the current educational plans of the states (Diskowski, 2005). In summary, the educational plans claim obligation. It is, however, open as to how this will be reached. In addition, currently no educational plan provides for external evaluation of its appropriate realization in the local practice. Thus, it is unclear how the educational plans fulfill the intended steering function.

The Transition from Kindergarten to Elementary School

The transition from Kindergarten to elementary school is one of the most long-lasting subjects in the discussion of the German educational system (Faust & Rossbach, 2004). During the 1960s and 1970s—a period called *Bildungsreform* (educational reform) in Germany—several model projects were conducted in order to facilitate this transition for the children. These model projects mainly focused on the 5-year-old children, the oldest age group in the classical Kindergarten age in Germany. Two types of models were considered:

- *Eingangsstufe* (school entrance class). In this type, the last year of
  Kindergarten is connected to the 1st grade of elementary school in
  order to combine educational methods of both systems within the
  elementary school. Children were sent to the school entrance class
  upon turning 5. They spent, in general, 2 years in this school entrance
  class in a mixed-age group before they passed over to 2nd grade.
  This school entry class was to reduce frictions that can commonly
  be observed in the course of transitions from one educational level
  to another, by leading from more play-oriented to more school-
  like learning experiences in one single educational setting (within
  elementary school).
- *Vorklasse* (preschool class; i.e., the model of the U.S. Kindergarten). The
  vorklasse at elementary school consists only of one preparatory school

year inserted before the usual elementary school. Children were sent to this preparatory class upon turning 5.

In both types of models, staff from Kindergarten as well as from elementary school worked together and supported the children individually and led them from preschool to school-like tasks and content. Various evaluation studies compared the effects of the stimulation of 5-year-old children in school entry classes, preparatory classes, and traditional Kindergarten (i.e., in mixed-age groups of about three age groups). Results from these evaluations were interpreted by educational and social politics (especially from the field of the organizations running the Kindergartens) as displaying equal effects in all types. With light reference to these results, the political decision was made to keep the 5-year-old children in the Kindergarten and not assign them to school entry classes or preparatory classes in elementary school. Yet when analyzing these results in more detail, there is doubt on this interpretation. There are indications pointing to certain advantages in the models of school entry class and preschool class (Fried, Rossbach, Tietze, & Wolf, 1992).

Since the transition from Kindergarten to elementary school is still considered a problematic transition for at least a group of children (in 2007, 4.8% of all children of the legal school entrance age delayed school start for 1 year), a new reform model has been developed in Germany (Autorengruppe Bildungsberichterstattung, 2008; Faust, 2006; Faust & Rossbach, 2004). Currently, 15 of the 16 states are testing a *neue schuleingangsstufe* (new school entry class), which is not designed to connect the two educational levels (Kindergarten and elementary school), but rather to rebuild the first two grades in elementary school. Still, the aim of this new school entrance class is to reduce friction between the two adjacent educational levels. Reducing the number of deferred enrollments, mixed-age grouping, and a variable time (1 to 3 years) spent in this class are the leading concepts. Children who need more time to learn, or who are not quite ready for school yet, can remain a third year in this class. To support these children in particular, it is recommended to involve specially trained personnel, who are not provided in all states. However, there is no homogeneous model of the neue schuleingangsstufe in Germany because the realization of the general idea is quite differently executed in the different states. The most prominent disadvantage in current studies is a widespread characteristic of German educational reforms: the lack of independent evaluation in most states. Thus, empirical knowledge about the effects of this new school entrance class is scarce. There are some indications that the proportion of students who spend 3 years in the new school entrance class is slightly lower than the usual proportion of students whose school start is delayed for 1 year. On the other side, the proportion of students who spend only 1 year in the new school entrance class is slightly higher than the usual proportion of students who start compulsory school 1 year earlier than expected according to their age. Because of the different realizations of the general idea of the neue schuleingangsstufe in the different German states—and, to some degree, a shift of the political attention to other areas of educational reform, such as educational plans, which comprise adjacent levels of the educational system or language diagnosis and language training for migrant children (Faust, 2006)—the further development of the neue schuleingangsstufe is unclear.

Recently, the idea of *Bildungshaeuser* (houses of education) for children from age 3 to 10 emerged. The main idea is to have closer local cooperation between Kindergarten and elementary school—not only to improve the transition phase but to include all age groups from 3 to 10 years old in a unified program. However, a more detailed concept has not yet been developed. In 2008, a large model program for developing and evaluating Bildungshaeuser has started in the state of Baden-Wuerttemberg.

The Kindergarten der Zukunft in Bavaria—KiDZ

In the "old" school entrance class, the last year of Kindergarten was connected to the 1st grade of elementary school in order to combine educational methods of both systems within the elementary school. Staff from both educational levels worked together in the old school entrance class. The "new" school entrance class is not designed to connect the two educational levels of Kindergarten and elementary school, but rather to rebuild the first two grades in elementary school. In general, only elementary school teachers—partly supported by auxiliary staff from the field of sociopedagogy—teach in the new school entrance class.

The idea to have staff from both Kindergarten and elementary school working together in one setting is central to a model project currently run in Bavaria: the *Kindergarten der Zukunft in Bayern—KiDZ* (Kindergarten of the future in Bavaria).[3] Staff from different professional levels—including an elementary school teacher and two differently trained Kindergarten teachers—cooperate in each KiDZ group (team teaching) and accompany children during the classical 3 Kindergarten years. The KiDZ groups are mixed-age groups with children from, in general, age 3 up to the age of compulsory schooling. The goal is to educate children more individually. After Kindergarten, KiDZ children move to a neue schuleingangsstufe (new school entrance class) and it is expected that a large proportion will only stay 1 year in the neue schuleingangsstufe before moving to grade 3. The two main goals of KiDZ are in line with the general considerations of reform of the German educational system: to put more emphasis on the promotion of individual competencies, especially with regard to language, early literacy, and numeracy; and to decrease the age when children finish school and, thus, allow an earlier entrance into the labor market. It is not assumed that all children only stay 1 year in the neue schuleingangsstufe. It is, however, expected to decrease the average number of years children spend in the formal school system.

The educational concept of the model project KiDZ does not follow one specific approach. Rather, it is based on the results of national and international programs and research, best practice, and the traditions of the German Kindergarten. The educational concept tries to incorporate different approaches and to develop units to support the acquisition of specific content knowledge like, for example, numeracy, language and early literacy, social and natural science, social behavior, creativity, music, and movement. The continuity with the traditions of the Kindergarten can be seen in that, for example, the concept and materials developed for the stimulation of mathematical competencies resemble very much the concept and materials developed by Friedrich Froebel about 160 years ago.

It is very important to note that the stimulation of the specific competencies of the children is not identical with traditional school lessons or working worksheets or training by use of computer programs. For children of this age group (starting with age 3), it seems much more reasonable to start with meaningful everyday situations in the KiDZ group—projects, problems, or play—and to actively use these situations to broaden the competencies of the children in specific areas. KiDZ tries to balance in its approach the use of such situations and the use of specific teacher-led efforts to stimulate the children. Both have to be meaningful for the children. In such a sense, the concept is child-oriented as well as subject-oriented.

No evaluation results for the KiDZ model project were available at the time of the writing of this chapter. In addition, it is uncertain whether the KiDZ model project in this form can be implemented on a broad scale in Bavaria, even if the evaluation results are very positive. In Bavaria, there are currently about 6,000 Kindergartens with about 16,000 groups. Thus, about 16,000 elementary teachers would be needed and would have to be financed for an implementation. Currently, the amount of financial resources needed considerably exceeds the resources available. Therefore, the main utilization of the results of the KiDZ model project can be seen in the development and testing of the educational approaches and in influencing a reform of teacher training for working in Kindergarten.

NOTES

1. From now on, the term *Kindergarten* is used as generic term for all institutional forms of early childhood care and education for children from age 3 up to starting elementary school.

2. Partly connected with the development of curricula is the discussion on raising the level of the teacher training for preschool settings to an academic level (technical college or university, as opposed to "Category 5 institutions," which are considered "lower" than technical college). This discussion is not addressed here.

3. The project is funded by the Bavarian ministry of education (*Bayerisches Staatsministerium für Unterricht und Kultus*), the Bavarian ministry of work and social welfare, families, and women (*Bayerisches Staatsministerium für Arbeit und Sozialordnung, Familie und Frauen*), and organizations of the Bavarian economy (*vbw—Vereinigung der Bayerischen Wirtschaft*, supported by the *Verband der Bayerischen Metall- und Elektroindustrie*), as well as by a Bavarian foundation focusing on education (*Stiftung Bildungspakt Bayern*). Currently, the model projects runs for 5 years in 10 *Kindergarten* groups, with children going to three associated elementary schools. The evaluation is located at the University of Bamberg.

REFERENCES

Autorengruppe Bildungsberichterstattung. (2008). *Bildung in Deutschland 2008: Ein indikatorengestuetzter Bericht mit einer Analyse zu Uebergaengen im Anschluss an den Sekundarbereich* [Education in Germany 2008: An indicator-based report]. Bielefeld: Bertelsmann.

Diskowski, D. (2005). Bildungsplaene fuer den Kindergarten: Abschied von der Unverbindlichkeit [Curricula for Kindergarten: Leaving informality?]. *Zukunfts-Handbuch Kindertageseinrichtungen, 43*.

Faust, G. (2006). Zum Stand der Einschulung und der neuen Schuleingangsstufe in Deutschland [School entry and the new school entrance class]. *Zeitschrift für Erziehungswissenschaft* [Journal of Education Science], *9*, 328–347.

Faust, G., & Rossbach, H. G. (2004). Der Uebergang vom Kindergarten in die Grundschule [The transition from Kindergarten to elementary school]. In L. Denner & E. Schumacher (Eds.), *Uebergaenge im Elementar- und Primarbereich reflektieren und gestalten. Beitraege zu einer grundlegenden Bildung* [Considering and arranging transitions between preschool and elementary school] (pp. 91–105). Bad Heilbrunn: Klinkhardt.

Fried, L., Rossbach, H. G., Tietze, W., & Wolf, B. (1992). Elementarbereich [Preschool education]. In K. Ingenkamp, R. S. Jaeger, H. Petillon, & B. Wolf (Eds.), *Empirische Paedagogik 1970–1990. Eine Bestandsaufnahme der Forschung in der Bundesrepublik Deutschland. Vol. 1* [A review of educational research in Germany] (pp. 197–263). Weinheim: Deutscher Studienverlag.

Herff, E. (1967). *Die Schulreife als paedagogisch-psychologisches Problem* [School readiness as educational-psychological problem]. Munich: Ernst Reinhardt Verlag.

Mader, J. (1989). *Schulkindergarten and Zurueckstellung. Zur Bedeutung schulisch-oekologischer Bedingungen bei der Einschulung* [Retention classes and delay of school start. Importance of school-ecological conditions when sending children to school]. Muenster: Waxmann.

OECD. (2004). *Die Politik der fruehkindlichen Betreuung, Bildung und Erziehung in der Bundesrepublik Deutschland: Ein Laenderbericht der Organisation fuer wirtschaftliche Zusammenarbeit und Entwicklung (OECD)* [Politics for early childhood care and education in the Federal Republic of Germany: A country report by the OECD]. Paris: Author.

Rossbach, H. G. (2001). Die Einschulung in den Bundeslaendern [Sending children to school in the States of Germany]. In G. Faust-Siehl & A. Speck-Hamdan (Eds.), *Schulanfang ohne Umwege* [Beginning school without detours] (pp. 145–174). Frankfurt: Grundschulverband—Arbeitskreis Grundschule.

Rossbach, H. G. (2003). Vorschulische Erziehung [Preschool education]. In K. S. Cortina, J. Baumert, J. A. Leschinsky, K. U. Mayer, & L. Trommer (Eds.), *Das Bildungswesen in der Bundesrepublic Deutschland. Strukturen und Entwicklung im Ueberblick* [The educational system in Germany: An overview of structures and developments] (pp. 252–284). Reinbek bei Hamburg: Rowohlt.

Rossbach, H. G., & Erning, G. (in preparation). *Uebergang vom Kindergarten in die Grundschule—eine unendliche Geschichte* [Transition from Kindergarten to school—An endless story].

Ruediger, D., Kormann, A., & Peez, H. (1976). *Schuleintritt und Schulfaehigkeit: Zur Theorie und Praxis der Einschulung* [School start and school readiness: Theory and practice of sending children to school]. Munich: Ernst Reinhardt.

Tietze, W., Rossbach, H. G., & Ufermann, K. (1989). Child care and early education in the Federal Republic of Germany. In P. P. Olmsted & D. P. Weikart (Eds.), *How nations serve young children: Profiles of child care and education in 14 countries* (pp. 39–85). Ypsilanti, MI: High/Scope Press.

CHAPTER 5

3- to 8-Year-Old Children in Japan
The Education System in Society

REIKO UZUHASHI

Japan consists of four principal islands on which 126 million people live within about 377,800 square kilometers. It is densely populated according to Western standards, and because most of the land is mountainous, people live just on the edges of the islands and in isolated small plains and basins. Japan is a nation poor in natural resources, and it depends mainly on imports from foreign countries for industrial materials.

BACKGROUND INFORMATION ABOUT JAPAN

A Brief History

In 1867 Japan bade farewell to its feudal economic and political systems controlled by the Tokugawa Shogunate and paved the way for the creation of a modern capitalistic nation under the strong initiative of the Meiji government. The process of this transition is called the Meiji Restoration. It brought revolutionary changes to Japan, which started with the coming of the Western powers.

Since 1867 over 140 years have passed. These years are divided into two periods, the first ending with the end of World War II in 1945 and the second beginning with the postwar period. From the time World War II ended until the Peace Treaty was signed in 1951, Japan was under the joint sovereignty of the Allied Forces and the Japanese government. During that time a range of innovative measures were implemented, including the establishment of the new Constitution. Japan became a democratic nation.

From 1951 until the mid-1970s there was remarkable economic growth, which went hand-in-hand with massive changes in industrial structure and in people's lives. Many people moved from rural areas to cities, where many large-scale firms were founded. This also resulted in major changes to family structure and to the traditional community.

People enjoyed Japan's strong economy for a while, and they became wealthy compared to earlier generations, but in 1990 the bubble burst and, since then, Japan has been suffering from a prolonged weak economy. In addition, in recent years the population has aged rapidly and fertility has declined sharply. This is becoming a more serious problem year by year.

3- to 8-Year-Old Children in Japan

Children in this age range are in kindergartens, nursery centers, and elementary schools. The schools are run under different political systems. Like elementary schools, kindergarten is under the authority of the Ministry of Education, Culture, Sports, Science, and Technology, and the nursery center is under the authority of the Ministry of Health, Labor, and Welfare.

Kindergarten is for 3- to 5-year-old children and is not compulsory, but is considered a part of the education system. It provides children with 1- to 3-year courses, 4 hours a day, 5 days a week during the school term. The kindergarten aims to help children to develop themselves mentally and physically through a sound educational environment under a regulated standard, which is, in other words, the national curriculum. The fee is the same for every child, but there are sometimes discounts for siblings. About 20% of kindergartens are run by local governments, and the rest are private. In 2003 the monthly costs paid by parents for public and private kindergarten were $57 and $183 respectively. Parents who send their children to private kindergartens get financial aid from the local government, so the real cost is less than $183 (Minervashobo, 2004).

Center-based day care is available for children under 6 who need child care so their parents can work. The certified nursery center is put in the framework of the child welfare system. It provides preschool education to 3- to 6-year-old children and, while not required to do so, may abide by the same standards as kindergartens. The fee depends on parents' income, children's age, the number of siblings, and where the family lives. For a 3-year-old, the monthly cost paid by parents is $230 on average. Private firms are subsidized by the local government, so the fee paid by parents is the same for public and private care (Minervashobo, 2004).

Legislation established both the regulated kindergarten and the certified nursery center in 1947. The kindergarten mainly provides educational programs, and the certified nursery center provides care and education programs. They are the main two alternatives to parental home-based care and supervision for preschool-age children.

The kindergarten enrollment rate grew dramatically until 1975 and has remained around 60%. Other children are in the nursery centers, so almost all preschool children in Japan have experiences of preschool education in some form (see Table 5.1). For many outside observers the public early childhood education and care (ECEC) system in Japan may appear quite generous (Boling, 1998).

TABLE 5.1. The Number of Children Enrolled in Preschool Institutions

Age (years)	Total number of children (thousands)	Nursery center		Kindergarten	
		Enrollment (thousands)	Percentage of total	Enrollment (thousands)	Percentage of total
under 3	3,625	399	11	–	–
0	1,198	46	3.8	–	–
1–2	2,427	353	14.6	–	–
3	1,209	377	31.2	322	26.6
4	1,259	829	65.8	742	58.9
5	1,302	–	–	843	64.7
Total 0–5	7,395	1,605	21.7	1,907	25.8

Source: Minervashobo, 1999

Since all children who have reached the age 6 are required to attend elementary school, 6- to 8-year-old children are in the first half of elementary school. Elementary schools are required to provide primary general education suited to the stage of mental and physical development. The 6 years of elementary school and 3 years of junior high school are compulsory, and are provided free at public schools. The regulated national curriculum is applied to both public schools and private ones.

A Brief History of the Modern School System

For about 250 years before the Meiji Restoration (1830s–1890s), the Tokugawa Shogunate maintained a closed-door policy and Japan enjoyed stability and peace as a whole society even though there was a strict class distinction among people. Each class had developed its own educational system, which means that distinctive schools were developed for each strata: the fief schools for the *samurai* (knighthood) and various kinds of private schools for commoners. The basis of people's enthusiasm for education was established gradually during this era.

The open-door policy was adopted in 1858. Under the Meiji Restoration the central government gave priority to survival as an independent country against the Western countries' great power. Since the modernization of the country and the establishment of strong national identity were urgent issues, the government introduced modern social and economic systems, including educational practices from Western countries. The policies went with the slogans of "Civilization and enlightenment," "Enriching the nation and building up a strong military," and "Encouragement and development of manufacturing industries."

The government had an enormous ambition to achieve the modernization of education. The combination of the original educational system that had been already developed during the Tokugawa Shogunate and educational ideas introduced from Western countries made the progress easy. As Japan had no experiences as a colony, there was no heritage from any suzerain country. Taking advantage of this freedom to select practices to emulate, the government took the model of the school system from the United States and took the centralization of the educational administration and school district system from France. The modern school system of Japan started in 1872 with the Educational Order Law.

After World War II, the Fundamental Law of Education and the School Education Law were enacted in 1947, and the 6-3-3-4–year system of school education was an effort to realize the principle of equal opportunity for education.

EARLY CHILDHOOD EDUCATION AND CARE SYSTEM

Since the mid-1960s the Japanese public ECEC system has expanded nationwide under the control of national and local governments. The regulated kindergarten and the certified nursery center have been the two major public ECEC forms in Japan. The government subsidizes both of them through a grants system. The nursery center was subsidized by the mandatory placement system until 1996.

Now, due to recent changes in the social climate, the ECEC system needs to be changed accordingly. Declining birth rate, increasing maternal employment, and welfare state restructuring have influenced the reorganization of the ECEC system. More attention has been focused on providing care for preschool children while their parents work, and on supporting stay-at-home mothers who are carrying the burden of childrearing.

Kindergarten

Kindergartens admit children from age 3 to 6, after which children enter elementary school. Kindergartens are run according to national standards by local governments or private firms. The minimum number of school weeks for kindergarten education is 39 weeks a year.

Kindergarten facilities are regulated by the Standards for the Establishment of Kindergartens. The standards prescribe the maximum number of children per class as 35, and at least one teacher must be placed in each class. The educational program is provided with the standards of the national curriculum, whose integral concept is based on the ideas of kindergarten developed by Froebel.

Kindergarten teachers are required to have relevant teacher certifications awarded by prefectural boards of education as provided for by the Education Personnel Certification Law. (Japan is divided into 47 prefectures, each of which is further divided into municipalities.) They complete at least a 2-year program at a university or junior college after graduating from high school at 18. Most kindergarten teachers are young, especially at private (usually not-for-profit) firms (see Table 5.2).

TABLE 5.2. Age of Kindergarten and Elementary School Teachers

| | KINDERGARTEN TEACHERS | | | | | | | | ELEMENTARY SCHOOL TEACHERS | |
| | Total | | National | | Municipal | | Private | | | |
Age	N	%	N	%	N	%	N	%	N	%
All	101,052	100.0	286	100.0	23,023	100.0	77,743	100.0	410,374	100.0
<25	39,258	38.8	5	1.7	2,065	9.0	37,183	47.8	11,819	2.9
25–29	17,939	17.8	55	19.2	2,388	10.4	15,496	19.9	47,328	11.5
30–34	6,645	6.6	63	22.0	1,902	8.3	4,680	6.0	62,015	15.1
35–49	8,103	8.0	49	17.1	4,150	18.0	3,904	5.0	85,017	20.7
40–44	9,135	9.0	32	11.2	5,356	23.3	3,747	4.8	78,562	19.1
45–49	7,833	7.8	35	12.2	4,132	17.9	3,666	4.7	56,918	13.9
50–54	3,896	3.9	26	9.1	1,668	7.2	2,202	2.8	34,440	8.4
55–59	2,763	2.7	20	7.0	945	4.1	1,798	2.3	30,757	7.5
60–64	2,087	2.1	1	0.3	341	1.5	1,745	2.2	3,429	0.8
over 65	3,393	3.4			76	0.3	3,317	4.3	89	0.0

Source: Minervashobo, 1999. Some entries are presented with shading to show the difference in ages of private, municipal, and national kindergarten teachers.

For the last several years, many kindergartens have provided extended-hour services for an extra fee to meet parents' needs. In 1993, 5.2% of public kindergartens and 29.5% of private kindergartens provided extended-hour services. By 2000, this had risen to 16.0% of public kindergartens and 71.5% of private kindergartens. In 52.3% of all kindergartens the extended-hour service is available 5 days per week, and in 41.8% of all until 6:00. Of private kindergartens, 7.5% accept children until 7:00 (Minervashobo, 2004).

Some working parents prefer kindergartens because they are more school-like or because the fees are cheaper for 3- to 5-year-olds, so in those cases kindergartens are expected to be custodial as well as educational. Extra educational programs like English conversation, piano lessons, or gymnastics are sometimes available for an extra fee for children who are present for an extended day. In some cases dinner is available.

Recently the government has started to give financial support to parents who have 3-year-old children and wish to put their children in kindergarten. Before that, kindergartens accepted children at the first April after their 3rd birthday. Now, once children turn 3 they can be accepted by kindergartens. The aim is to support mothers who are worried about children's social development because there are no same-age children around due to the decreasing number of children. Some mothers are isolated while raising young children. Kindergartens are motivated to provide early enrollment so that they do not lose children to other kindergartens that do.

Kindergarten is now deemed to fulfill an important role as an institution that provides custodial care for preschool children.

The Certified Nursery Center

The certified nursery center is the most desired option for working parents who wish to put their children into child care. At the moment there are long waiting lists for enrollment in certified nursery centers, which is called the Waiting Children Issue.

In the mid-1960s the certified nursery center system assumed its current form. In 1961 the procedures and conditions for a child's admission to a nursery center were established, and in 1965 Guidelines for Nursery Center Childcare were introduced.

Nursery centers admit children from birth to age 6. They typically provide care 8 hours per day year-round. Usually extended-hours service is available. Children may need child care because parents work outside the home or are unable to provide proper care due to disability or illness. For 3- to 6-year-old children educational programs are provided, with standards based on the national curriculum for kindergarten students.

All nursery teachers are required to be qualified as nursery workers. For that qualification it is necessary to complete a 2-year course at a university or college approved by the government or to pass an examination offered by prefectural governments. Qualified nursery workers often also have kindergarten teacher certificates.

Nursery centers' facilities are regulated by the Standards for the Establishment of the Nursery Center. The ratio of children/nursery workers is 3:1 for children under 1, 6:1 for 1- to 2-year-olds, 20:1 for 3-year-olds, and 30:1 for 4- to 6-year-olds.

For the last several years in some cities, privatization of public nursery centers has increased, and private nursery centers have been encouraged to accept infants and toddlers and to offer extended-hours service. Also, the government encourages nursery centers to accept children 11 hours or more per day.

Japanese social security underwent a thorough reform, and the reform process is still ongoing. Some critics have described this process as "the complete elimination of welfare." But the reality is not so simple, because the motive for reform is twofold. One factor is that owing to financial tightening, throughout the 1980s and 1990s every field faced financial problems. At the same time, Japan is seeking to prepare for the onset of a rapidly aging society. Measures have been implemented in the area of pensions and health services where the keynote is retrenchment; and in the field of personal social services new measures for financing have been implemented aiming to expand benefits to more beneficiaries, particularly among the elderly, as represented by the introduction of the Elderly Care Services Insurance Scheme (Ministry of Health, Labor, and Welfare, 1999).

As mentioned earlier, the certified nursery center system used to be operated within the framework of a mandatory placement system. Its implementation was strictly based on the idea that the state has the legal obligation to place a child in a nursery center once the child's need for care is proven. Although financial support still remains, the government no longer has the responsibility for providing child care. Child welfare reform legislation was introduced in 1996 as part of a larger welfare state restructuring project that has been taking place since the 1980s.

Children Waiting for Child Care

There were 39,545 children counted as waiting children as of April 1, 1998 (Ministry of Health, Labor, and Welfare, 1999). The story was different from region to region and by age of children. In a big city like Kawasaki one-fourth of the children who had applied for child care were on waiting lists, but the Japanese government said that nationally there are still places available for children.

As for the nationwide supply-and-demand situation, the total capacity of certified nursery centers in 1998 was 1.92 million, while the number of children actually served was 1.69 million. Thus the occupancy rate was 88%, so it seemed that supply exceeded demand on a national level (Ministry of Health, Labor, and Welfare, 1999).

The fact is that there are serious shortages of places for infants and toddlers and, on the other side, more places than needed for 3- to 5-year-old children. There was a huge gap between what parents required and what was available. For some time it seemed that the government was reluctant to recognize the gap, but on May 6, 2001, Japanese prime minister Junichiro Koizumi issued a statement challenging the waiting children issue and declaring the expansion of child care places, which is called the *Strategy for Zero Waiting Children* (Koizumi, 2003). In October 2000 it was calculated that the occupancy rate was up to 99%. The fact is that almost half of all nursery centers accept more children than the regulated capacity (Nursery centers are full, 2001).

The Uncertified Nursery

There is a third big group of child care facilities that are called uncertified nurseries. They cannot meet minimum licensing standards for any number of reasons, including unqualified staff, poor equipment, lack of space, and insufficient adult/child ratio. Uncertified nurseries may be expensive due to lack of government subsidization, but very often there is no choice for the parents of waiting children.

Uncertified nursery centers often offer more flexible hours, including evening and overnight child care, to meet parents' needs. Almost all the certified nursery centers provide child care only for parents who work ordinary work hours on a full-time basis, so they make no sense for parents who work evening or night shifts or work part-time. Some uncertified nurseries are operated at workplaces.

Baby hotels are uncertified nurseries that provide evening, overnight, or all-day care on a full- or part-time basis. They gained a lot of public attention because of the deaths and accidents that occurred at these facilities in the 1970s. Baby hotels are often used for infant care and, because of the generally inferior quality of these facilities, have become an issue of public concern, which has been recognized as the "baby hotel issue" since the 1980s.

Including baby hotels, many uncertified nurseries are run entirely on parents' contributions. Very often parents are faced with expensive fees and the children suffer from poor-quality service.

The Declining Birth Rate

In 1990 the Japanese government formally expressed its concern over the declining birth rate for the first time, more than 40 years after the birth rate started to decline in the mid-1940s. In 1990 the Minister of Health and

Welfare reported a total fertility rate of 1.57 for the year 1989 (Ministry of Health, Labor, and Welfare, 1999). It marked the lowest fertility rate in Japan since the war. This caused anxiety among politicians and government bureaucrats (the so-called "1.57 shock"). This broke the psychological barrier established in 1965 when the national fertility rate dropped from 2.14 to 1.58 within a year in reaction to the particularly bad luck associated with that year according to the Chinese astrological calendar[1] (Kashiwame, 1997). The low birth rate is related to future economic and social development in the rapidly aging society. Considering increasing maternal employment, the Ministry of Health and Welfare launched the "Five-year Program of Emergency Measures for Nursery Care and Other Related Matters" in 1994 to improve day care services in conjunction with the Labor, Construction, and Education Ministries. It is called the "Angel Plan" (Table 5.3). The Angel Plan aimed for ambitious child care expansion and has achieved a certain amount of it. In 1999 and 2004 it was revised with new goals.

In 1996 child welfare reform legislation was introduced as part of a larger welfare state restructuring project that has been taking place since the 1980s. The 1.57 shock and the child welfare reform legislation are the watersheds for the development of the Japanese public child care system. Current reforms like these may seem to signify a progressive step toward socialization of child care. Traditionally, child care was managed as a private matter. Mothers were expected to assume all responsibilities for childrearing, but this has become very difficult due to changes in society. The government now says that childrearing responsibilities should be shared among families, communities, and professional institutions.

ELEMENTARY SCHOOL

The elementary school is monitored (given guidance and advice) by each level of government: central, prefectural, and municipal. Each prefecture and municipality has its own Board of Education, which monitors the elementary school directly.

At the central government level the Elementary and Secondary Education Bureau is responsible for:

- establishing curriculum standards in elementary schools as well as other schools, including the kindergarten
- the free provision and authorization of textbooks
- the system for local education
- legal standards for class size, staffing numbers for schools, and the payment of school staff

TABLE 5.3. Expansion of Nursery Care of Other Early Childhood Services, 1995–1999

Category	FY1995 budget	FY1996 budget	FY1997 budget	FY1998 budget	FY1999 budget
Expansion in nursery center operation expenses and infant admission capacity	466,000 persons	489,000 persons	512,000 persons	535,000 persons	584,000 persons
Development of multifunction nursery centers	200 locations	200 locations	300 locations	282 locations (585 locations supplemented)	365 locations
Promotion of extended nursery care	2,530 locations	2,830 locations	4,000 locations	6,000 locations	7,000 locations
Promotion of temporary nursery care	600 locations	600 locations	800 locations	1,000 locations	1,500 locations
Community centers to support child care	354 locations	400 locations	600 locations	840 locations (including 200 small centers)	1,500 locations (including 900 small centers)
Afterschool sound childrearing program	5,220 locations	6,000 locations	6,900 locations	7,900 locations	9,000 locations
Infant health support temporary care program	40 locations	50 locations	100 locations	150 locations	450 locations

Source: Ministry of Health, Labor and Welfare, 1999,
http://www1.mhlw.go.jp/english/wp_5/vol2/p2c8.html

After World War II, important education laws such as the Fundamental Law of Education and the School Education Law were established. The new educational system was created, espousing respect for individual dignity and equal opportunities as its main ideals. The new education system takes a single-track format, the so-called 6-3-3-4 system, which was adapted to provide uniform education for all citizens. The first 9 years of education are compulsory.

The new system began under very difficult conditions after the war, but by the middle of the 1950s, the compulsory education system had stabilized. Access to it was secured nationwide, supported by people's enthusiasm for education and the efforts of people involved in education. However, the compulsory education system was instituted without adequate facilities and teachers. Teachers' salaries were somewhat stabilized with the law in 1952; one-half of the salary of each teacher in the compulsory education system would be paid by the National Treasury. The government began to subsidize teaching materials and classroom equipment in 1953 based on the law as well.

The government set up the Course of Study as the standard for curriculum, and authorization of textbooks is to be made based on it. The course of study has been revised roughly every 10 years to adapt to the changes in the society and economy. As a result of the introduction of the Educational Personnel Securing Law, teachers' salaries have risen.

CHARACTERISTICS OF EDUCATION

The Enthusiasm for Education

The entry rate to higher education institutions is still more or less on the rise, reaching 72.9% in 2003, and 74.2% for females. Looking at the entry rate to university and junior college (including those retaking university entrance exams), an upward trend was sustained until recently, when the rate flattened. In 2003 the rate was 49.0%, and 48.3% for females (Minervashobo, 2004).

People's enthusiasm for education does not always result in success. The employment rate for new university graduates (undergraduates) has been in decline since 1991, dropping to a record low of 55.1% in 2003 (Ministry of Health, Labor, and Welfare, 2004).

People's enthusiasm for education has a historical background and is combined with a strong desire to see children climb up the social ladder to get better jobs, enjoy better living standards, and get better life security compared to the parents' own generation. Education is the only strategy available to most people for rising socially. Such desires were fulfilled by companies' lifetime employment policies under the good economy. Students were expected just to show evidence of their general ability, which means attending good universities and understanding group cooperation, hard work, and perseverance. Companies afforded generous training opportunities to employees, but now things have changed after the end of the strong economy in the early 1990s.

High Ratio of Private Schools

The government budget has never matched people's enthusiasm for education. There has been a gap between them, where the government's supplying of education has not met public demand. To narrow the gap, private firms have established various kinds and levels of school, junior college, and university to absorb people's educational enthusiasm, especially in the area of higher education (see Figure 5.1). There is a wide diversity among the private institutions in terms of quality.

Influence and Pressure from Western Countries

Japan is always greatly influenced by foreign countries, and very often has been given opportunities for changes: the introduction of the modern education system in the Meiji era, educational reforms during the occupation period, recommendations from the Organization of Economic Cooperation and Development (OECD) in 1970, and now the results of international academic ability competitions like the Program for International Student Assessment (PISA).

FIGURE **5.1. Distribution of Student Enrollment: National, Municipal, and Private**

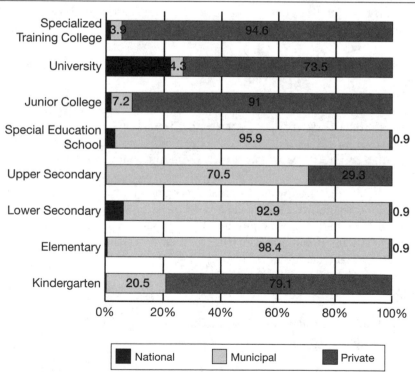

Source: Ministry of Education, Culture, Sports, Science and Technology, 2003

PROSPECTS

The Need for an Integrated Preschool System

Although child care services are expanding rapidly, with generous subsidies from the government, there still remains a gap between parents' needs and the availability of services. Parent demand outpaces the expansion of supply. The waiting children issue has not been resolved yet, and it is related to the uncertified nursery issue, like the baby hotel issue that has remained unresolved since the 1980s.

The quality of preschool education varies at both the kindergarten and nursery center. There is quite a diversity of methods, materials, equipment, and teacher salaries. The national curriculum provides only fundamental principles.

The dual system of education and care for preschool-aged children makes it difficult for parents to arrange coherent provision for their children. The task of Japan's ECEC policies is to establish the standards for integrated education and care service, give parents appropriate information about ECEC, and ensure its provision for every parent and child.

In the future it is desirable that free preschool education for 3- to 5-year-old children be available for every child.

Work and Life Balance of Parents

Successive Japanese governments have established education and child care policies based on traditional family values and gender codes, with the idea of a "Japanese welfare regime," which means that women are expected not only to provide care for the family but to discipline and educate children properly by themselves (Brinton, 1993; Peng, 2002; Uzuhashi, 2001). Now many women are well educated and accustomed to equal opportunities in the school system, and under the recession women's employment rate is rising. Gradually, living with the old traditional family values has become very hard. The traditional family and community are diminishing. We now need to provide emotional and social security for children, and give them the basis of learning, in the context of these new social relations and structures.

"Academic Ability" and Proper Educational Practice

The ministry of education provides comprehensive policies to greatly improve "academic ability" with five aims:

- Well-established basics and fundamentals
- Thinking ability, expressive ability, problem-solving ability
- Desire to continue to study throughout a lifetime

- Development of special talents of the individual student
- Vibrant intellectual curiosity and studiousness (Ministry of Education, Culture, Sports, Science and Technology, n.d.)

This policy itself should be acceptable to everyone, but will it become reality? There are too many critics, from government ministers to laypeople, to be able to come to a consensus and create effective practice. Everybody is a kind of education expert, based on their own educational background, and they trust their own opinions and feelings too much. The media do not always promote the most well-founded opinion. Sometimes teachers' opinions from the field are ignored. We must listen to teachers' voices.

NOTE

1. This year was notorious as the year of the fire-breathing horse (*hinoe-uma*). It is believed that girls born in that year will shorten their husbands' lives. Such years occur once every 60 years; in the 20th century there was only one, in 1966.

REFERENCES

Boling, P. (1998). Family policy in Japan. *Journal of Social Policy, 27*(2), 173–190.

Brinton, C. (1993). *Women and the economic miracle: Gender and work in postwar Japan.* Berkeley: University of California Press.

Kashiwame, R. (1997). *Jido Fukushi Kaikaku to Jissitaisei* [Child welfare reform and its system of implementation]. Kyoto: Minervashobo.

Koizumi, J. (2003, September 26). General Policy Speech by Prime Minister Junichiro Koizumi to the 157th Session of the Diet. Retrieved May 15, 2008, from http://www.mofa.go.jp/announce/pm/koizumi/state0926.html

Minervashobo. (1999). *Saisin Hoiku Shiryousyu* [Latest statistics and documents on Child-care in Japan]. Kyoto, Japan: Author.

Minervashobo. (2004). *Saisin Hoiku Shiryousyu* [Latest statistics and documents on Child-care in Japan]. Kyoto, Japan: Author.

Ministry of Education, Culture, Sports, Science and Technology. (n.d.). *Formal education: Elementary and secondary education.* Retrieved May 15, 2008, from http://www.mext.go.jp/english/org/f_formal.htm

Ministry of Education, Culture, Sports, Science and Technology. (2003). *School basic survey.* Tokyo: Author.

Ministry of Health, Labor, and Welfare. (1999). *Annual report on health and welfare: 1989–1999 social security and national life.* Tokyo: Author. Retrieved May 15, 2008, from http://www1.mhlw.go.jp/english/wp_5/vol2/p2c8.html

Ministry of Health, Labor, and Welfare. (2004). White paper on the labour economy 2004. Tokyo: Author. Retrieved May 15, 2008, from http://www.mhlw.go.jp/english/wp/l-economy/2004/index.html

Nursery centers are full: Government research in the last year. (2001, October 27). *Asahi Newspaper*, p. 29.

Peng, I. (2002). Gender and generation: Japanese child care and the demographic crisis. In S. Michel & R. Mahon (Eds.), *Child care policy at the crossroads: Gender and welfare state restructuring* (pp. 31–56). New York: Routledge.

Uzuhashi, T. (2001). Japan: Bidding farewell to the welfare society. In P. Alcock & G. Craig (Eds.), *International social policy* (pp. 104–123). Basingstoke, UK: Palgrave.

CHAPTER 6

Drawing Threads Together

The Development of
Early Education in New Zealand

MICHAEL GAFFNEY

New Zealand is a small island nation located at the bottom of the South Pacific 1,200 miles southeast of Australia. The country is similar in size and population to Colorado, with a land area of 268,021 square kilometres and a population of 4,115,771 (est. July 2007, Central Intelligence Agency, 2007). The country's political system uses a parliamentary democracy, with the British monarch as a nominal head of state and a prime minister as head of government. This system has been in place since 1852. Significant changes over time included the development of provincial government until 1876, during which time the provision of education varied according to provincial resources. New Zealand was given independence as a dominion in 1907 and dropped the two-house system of parliament in 1951. This means that changes in law are the responsibility of the current government, which has the majority of votes in the house of representatives.

British colonization began in the early 1800s, and New Zealand originally came under the authority of the governor of New South Wales in Australia before being established as separate colony in 1840. Formal colonization in New Zealand was different from previously established means of conquest. In 1840 a treaty was signed by many of the tribes that made up the local indigenous people called Māori. The Treaty of Waitangi has received new official recognition over the last 30 years, and while not forming the basis for a constitution, it is seen as a founding document of New Zealand. The notion of partnership in the treaty between the Crown and Māori has been used to legitimise the ongoing government resourcing for Māori in education, health, and welfare.

THE CURRENT SCHOOL SYSTEM

A Ministry of Education based in the nation's capital of Wellington administers the school system. This ministry has the overall responsibility for formal early childhood education (ECE), compulsory education, and tertiary education (Ministry of Education, 2003). There are separate agencies responsible for qualifications, teacher registration, tertiary management, and school and early childhood review. All organizations report to the same minister of education, except the Education Review Office. The current setup was established in 1989 after a comprehensive review called *Tomorrow's Schools*, which saw the separation of policy provision, service provision, and review mechanisms. Education legislation is passed by the national parliament and makes provision for the addition of regulations and rules. The current mission in national education policy "is to raise achievement and reduce disparity. Our overarching outcome is to build a world-leading education system that equips all New Zealanders with the knowledge, skills and values to be successful citizens in the twenty-first century" (Ministry of Education, 2007a, p. 11).

Each of New Zealand's 2,600 state schools are managed by their own Boards of Trustees, whether it be a school with 12 students or 3,000. These boards, designated by legislation, are made up of elected parent representatives, a staff representative, a student representative (if a secondary school), and the school's principal. These boards have legislative responsibilities designated by the National Education Guidelines, which form the basis of the charter between the school and its community and the New Zealand government. These are often referred to as "the NEGs and NAGs [National Administration Guidelines]." Boards, as well as having to ensure that they meet their obligations according to the Education Act of 1989, have another 20 pieces of legislation that they must take into account because as well as being responsible for teaching and learning, they are also responsible for financial and property management and being a "good employer" (Ministry of Education, 2007b).

The government uses the curriculum framework (Ministry of Education, 1993) to guide teaching, learning, and assessment. There are curriculum statements for seven essential learning areas: language, mathematics, science, technology, social sciences, the arts (visual arts, music, dance, and drama) and health and physical well-being. The curriculum framework also promotes eight sets of essential skills: communications, numeracy, information, problem-solving, self-management and competitive, social and cooperative, physical, and work and study skills, as well as attitudes and values associated with each learning area. The Ministry of Education released a new draft curriculum in 2006. It is up to schools to develop their own curriculum plan and means of schoolwide assessment.

There are no national requirements in terms of time, texts, or resources to be used for particular curriculum areas. In the National Administration Guidelines, which form part of the National Education Guidelines, there are requirements for each board, through the principal and staff, to develop and implement teaching and learning programmes:

a. to provide all students in Years 1–10 with opportunities to achieve for success in all the essential learning and skill areas of the New Zealand curriculum;
b. giving priority to student achievement in literacy and numeracy, especially in Years 1–4.

It is the responsibility of the Education Review Office to ensure that each school is meeting expectations around a board's legal responsibilities. Each school and early childhood service is inspected every 3 years, with reports made publicly available (see http://www.ero.govt.nz).

State schooling is available to students from when they turn 5 until the end of the year in which they turn 19. The compulsory age of enrollment is age 6 to 16. Children move through year levels at school, from Year 1 when they first enter to Year 13. The vast majority of children start school at age 5 even though it is not compulsory until they turn 6. The majority of schools are Year 1–6 primary (elementary) schools, but in smaller towns and rural locations schools might be full primary Year 1–8 or area/composite schools Year 1–13. There are approximately 750,000 students in elementary and secondary education being taught by some 53,000 teachers in 2,100 primary (Year 1–8) and 500 secondary (Year 9–13) or composite (Year 1–13) schools.

New Zealand's children of indigenous descent, the Māori, make up 20% of the school population. The majority of private schools are religious in nature, with Catholic schools making up about 10% of the schools in New Zealand. The Catholic schools joined the state system in 1975 through a process of "integration." This allowed private schools to maintain their "special character" and draw on state funds, in exchange for which they are now required to teach the national school curriculum. This is not to say that they were not teaching it to begin with, as evidenced by the near-universal use of the state exam system across the private school sector. Catholic schools and other state-integrated schools retain ownership of their school property but receive funding for salaries, operating expenses, and property maintenance. There is also a restriction on the amount of fees that can be charged limited to that required for capital works and maintenance. This leaves some 5% of schools, which are private, accounting for some 3% of the school population. Private schools have recently received between 25 and 40% of what state schools receive, depending on the age level of the students although this amount has decreased with the current government, which is less enthusiastic about supporting private schools. There is no requirement to teach the state school curriculum, but they are still visited by the Education Review Office to ensure that legislative requirements are met and a programme of education is provided.

National exams are available in the last 3 years of schooling, and national assessment is used to provide data on national trends in educational performance.

Each year 10% of schools have their Year 4 and Year 8 students participate in curriculum activities so that over 4 years data are collected on all curriculum areas (see http://nemp.otago.ac.nz). The assessment includes group work and hands-on activities that require videotaping for analysis. A new programme of pencil-and-paper testing has been developed for Years 4–11 around numeracy and literacy, called asTTLe (Assessment Tools for Teaching and Learning). In this programme teachers can put together tests from a bank of items and then compare their students' results with the national norms established earlier. These assessment items are provided in both English and Mäori. Mäori immersion schools are called Kura Kaupapa. There have been several school entry assessments developed in the areas of literacy, oral language, and numeracy. These are not compulsory, but the schools are invited to submit their results in order to give a picture of school entry skill levels of students. When students turn 6 many are assessed for their progress in reading as part of the Reading Recovery programme. Those who are not meeting school standards may receive extra assistance. Not all schools use this programme.

THE CURRENT EARLY CHILDHOOD SYSTEM

New Zealand early childhood education (ECE) systems are being developed within a 10-year plan called *Pathways to the Future—2002–2012* (Ministry of Education, 2002). The plan has three goals:

- Increase participation in quality ECE services
- Improve quality of ECE services
- Promote collaborative relationships.

The plan includes a review of funding, with the provision of 20 hours per week of free education and care for 3- and 4-year-old children that began in 2007; a review of regulations, which is under way and due for release in 2007; and a raising of qualification requirements for all teachers so that by the end of the 10-year plan all teachers will have a minimum of a 3-year diploma and be registered in the same way that schoolteachers are.

One of the aims of the plan is to provide a system that maintains and supports the diverse range of services currently available to parents and families. The plan describes these as:

- *Education and care centres* provide either sessional, all-day, or flexible-hours programmes for children from birth to school age. They may be privately owned, non-profit, community-based, or operated as an adjunct to the main purpose of a business or organisation (e.g., a crèche at a university or polytechnic college). These centres include a small but increasing number of specific Māori-immersion education and care centres, and Pacific Island Education and Care Centres.

- *Home-based services* comprise a cluster (network) of home-based caregivers operating under the supervision of a coordinator. The coordinator places children with caregivers in approved homes for an agreed number of hours per week.
- *Kindergartens* generally operate sessional early childhood education for children between the ages of 3 and 5.
- *Kōhanga Reo* provide programmes totally in Te Reo and Tikanga, Māori for mokopuna and their whānau from birth to school age.[1]
- *Licence-exempt play groups* are community-based groups of parents and children who meet for one to three sessions per week.
- *Parent support and development programmes* aim to improve health, social, and educational outcomes by helping to build parenting capability (e.g., PAFT [Parents as First Teachers], HIPPY [Home Instruction Programme for Preschool and Year 1 Youngsters]).
- *Play centers are collectively supervised* and managed by parents for children up to age 5.
- *The Correspondence School* provides distance ECE for children ages 3 to 5 who are unable to attend an ECE service because of isolation, illness, or other special needs. (Ministry of Education, 2002)

Unlike schools, these services (except the Correspondence School) are not state-owned or -run. The legislation requires that they must be licensed in order to operate as a service. To access state funding the service must also include a charter that contains extra requirements in terms of educational pro-vision. These rules are called Desirable Objectives and Practices (DOPs, the equivalent of NEGs and NAGs for schools). The DOPs specify curriculum provision, communication with parents, and administrative requirements for appropriate financial and personnel management. Although the government may make a significant contribution to funding the setup of centres, state con-trol is restricted to legislation and funding. The current DOPs require that ser-vices use the New Zealand early childhood curriculum or something similar. The strategic plan intends to make the curriculum compulsory. It is expected that the DOPs will be replaced by criteria that are specific to service types as listed above.

The development of the early childhood curriculum *Te Whāriki* (Ministry of Education, 1996) was a key feature of the 1990s early childhood policy. This Māori term refers to the woven mat, which is the metaphor used to promote the elements of the curriculum. The curriculum is made up of four principles and five strands.

The four principles are:

1. *Empowerment*: The early childhood curriculum empowers the child to learn and grow.
2. *Holistic Development*: The early childhood curriculum reflects the holistic way children learn and grow.
3. *Family and Community*: The wider world of family and community is an integral part of the early childhood curriculum.
4. *Relationships*: Children learn through responsive and reciprocal relationships with people, places, and things. (p. 14)

The five strands are:

1. *Well-being*–Children experience an environment where their health is promoted, their emotional well-being is nurtured, and they are kept safe from harm.
2. *Belonging*–Children and their families experience an environment where connecting links with the family and wider world are affirmed and extended; they know they have a place; they feel comfortable with the routines, customs, and regular events; and they know the limits and boundaries of acceptable behaviour.
3. *Contribution*–Children experience an environment where there are equitable opportunities for learning, irrespective of gender, ability, age, ethnicity or background; they are affirmed as individuals; and they are encouraged to learn with and alongside others.
4. *Communication*–Children experience an environment where they develop nonverbal and verbal communication skills for a range of purposes; they experience stories and symbols of their own and other cultures; and they develop different ways to be creative and expressive.
5. *Exploration*–Children experience an environment where their play is valued as meaningful learning; they gain confidence and control of their bodies; they learn strategies for active exploration, thinking, and reasoning; and they develop working theories for making sense of their social, physical, and material world. (Ministry of Education, 1996, pp. 15–16)

In order to support the diversity of services using the document and build on the sociocultural theoretical framework the curriculum took on a form that is process-oriented rather than content-specific. This means that it looks more like the essential skills within the national curriculum framework rather than the essential learning areas. There is also a separate section written in

Māori for Kohanga Reo and other Māori language-immersion services. This section is not just replication of what is written in English. For example, the importance of *wairua* (spirituality) is acknowledged, which is absent in the English part.

As *Te Whāriki* was the first national curriculum for early childhood in New Zealand and services were being required to use it, the Ministry of Education started to fund a lot more professional development. This was something that had been available in the compulsory sector for quite some time but was new for early childhood. The bulk of the resources were put into whole-centre or service development on the basis that educator practices would not change unless teams of educators changed together. The tension that arose was that facilitators were providing a very bottom-up approach to organisational development at the same time they were supporting the implementation of national policy (Gaffney, 2003). This format had been used in the compulsory sector, but within the ECE sector the diversity of services meant that the tensions were more apparent. The feature of the curriculum that reduced the tension was the extensive 3-year consultation and development phase that allowed the diverse range of services the opportunities to see themselves represented in the curriculum (Smith, 2003). Such a consultation period had not been available for the development of school curriculum statements, where turnaround between drafts and final statements was between 6 and 12 months.

One way of improving the acceptability of the curriculum was to keep the focus on the learner rather than the educator. The term *educator* is used so that it can include both teachers and parents. Parents make up the bulk of the adults who support children in Kōhanga Reo and Playcentres. The focus on learning rather than teaching has been one of the criticisms of the curriculum, where the role of the educator must be inferred (Meade, 2002), with the result that it does not encourage educators to "articulate their pedagogical practice to parents, whānau [extended family], and community" (p. 15).

With the curriculum in place for nearly 10 years, the attention of national resourcing has been turned to assessment within the curriculum. Margaret Carr, who was one of the co-authors of *Te Whāriki*, has been working on an assessment framework called learning stories (Carr, 2001). The strands of the curriculum are now seen in the assessment framework. If children are showing a sense of belonging, then they will start to *take an interest;* if their well-being is nurtured, then they will *become involved;* if they start to contribute to centre activities, then they will *take responsibility* for themselves and others; if they are communicating, then they will be *expressing a point of view;* and if they are exploring, then they will *persist with difficulty, challenge, and uncertainty.* The development of learning stories includes a focus on hearing the voice of the child, educator, and parent/caregiver within the assessment process, based on a narrative approach. The next stage in the development of assessment across the range of services has been the publication of *Kei Tua o te Pae: Assessment for Learning: Early Childhood Exemplars* (Ministry of Education, 2005). The key words being explored are *noticing, recognizing,* and *responding.* The focus is on listening to the child, reflecting the complexity of early childhood pedagogy, and acknowledging that educators are usually working in teams.

As part of the strategic plan there is a strategy to "Promote coherence of education between birth and 8 years." Aspects of this include:

- promoting better understanding between ECE teachers and primary teachers about the links between *Te Whāriki* and the New Zealand Curriculum Framework
- promoting better understanding between ECE teachers and primary teachers about the pedagogical approaches in ECE and schools
- distributing information about effective transition from ECE to school practices. (Ministry of Education, 2002)

Work on developing this program is slow because the two sectors have not had a history of interaction. Some preservice teacher training institutions are now offering Diplomas of Teaching for birth to age 8 where graduates are qualified to teach in either the early childhood sector or the primary sector. Primary and early childhood teachers now belong to the same "union," the New Zealand Education Institute, which has increased interaction, and the development of pay parity between the kindergarten service and primary school teachers has further aligned the professions. Primary school teachers received pay parity with secondary school teachers a few years earlier, and it is hoped that the new funding frameworks will allow teachers in education and care centres to move to pay parity. The nation has an obligation to schoolteachers and kindergarten teachers as part of the State Sector Act. Even though the Ministry of Education is not the employer of teachers (that is the role of Boards of Trustees and the management of early childhood services), it is able to negotiate with the union for salaries and conditions. Only 10% of education and care centers negotiate with the union, which leaves the Ministry of Education without a mechanism for negotiating pay parity within New Zealand's current employment legislation.

The review of the New Zealand curriculum framework may also allow more alignment with *Te Whāriki.* As a result of the curriculum, stocktaking work is beginning around developing core competencies within curriculum areas that might allow a more integrated curriculum to be developed in schools. This has disappeared within the current framework and accountability systems. The reemergence of inquiry-based learning using such models as Costa's 16 habits of mind (Costa & Kallick, 2000) means that school teaching practices may well start to look like those being promoted by *Te Whāriki.*

THE HISTORY OF THE DEVELOPMENT OF SCHOOLING

The first attempts at school began with the missionaries who took it upon themselves to "civilise" the natives. The idea was that the parents could be reached through their children (May, 2003). The system of colonisation was based on organized settlements from England and Scotland, where money had been allocated for schools and churches. Schools were not always the outcome, and in some settlements schools began on the immigrant boats during the voyage, which would take 3 months (May, 2004).

The development of provincial government in 1852 meant that the level of schooling available ranged from nonexistent to free schooling. It was the return to national administration of education in 1876, with the abolition of provincial government, that saw the first Education Act in 1877, which included compulsory schooling from ages 7 to 12 and later free schooling from ages 5 to 15. While the new arrangement was based on compulsion, the resources to make this happen were inadequate. Attendance was only required for half the days that a school was open, leaving families to decide how important education was, relative to the other demands of life (New Zealand National Commission for UNESCO, 1952). Subsequent acts of Parliament slowly raised the age for free schooling to include secondary education in 1914, and reduced the minimum age for attendance to 6 in 1964. The UNESCO report says that the habit of school attendance was so well established by the early 1900s that children were attending for the all the years for which it was free rather than merely for what was compulsory. Initial achievement in primary schools was based on a National Certificate of Proficiency, which was dropped in 1936.

THE HISTORY OF THE DEVELOPMENT OF EARLY CHILDHOOD EDUCATION

May (1997) records the many attempts to establish kindergartens for the purposes of reducing the number of children on the streets having to occupy their own time as well as the smaller number of attempts to establish crèches for children whose parents were working. The first system of free kindergartens for 3- to 5-year-olds began in Dunedin in 1899 and spread through out the country over the next 20 years, supported by small amounts of government funding. The system is now well established in New Zealand for 3- and 4-year-olds, although the current system of licensing allows 2-year-olds to attend, which in some kindergartens can have a significant impact on the provision of services. This has occurred where, in order to maintain sustainability, the kindergarten has accepted younger children in order to maximise the number of children upon which funding is based.

World War II saw a new demand for child care and family support. This led to the development of parent-led Playcentres. Teachers are not necessary to the organization of the Playcentre. Rather, adults work as a cooperative to provide the number of sessions each week that people feel is desirable. These centres are now struggling to attract parents to support the system, because it is now very common for both parents to work and families are smaller than in the past. So even when families participate, they do not have the number of children to sustain the relationship with the Playcentre compared to 50 years ago.

The demand for child care has been associated with the development of the women's movement in the 1970s. With increasing numbers of mothers taking on some form of work, the demand for care and education went beyond what was available from kindergartens and Playcentres. Child care was originally the responsibility of the Department of Social Welfare. In 1986 New Zealand was one of the first countries to integrate the responsibility for all early childhood services within the education system (Smith, 2003). Education and care centres, as they are officially called today, are the largest group of licensed centres available in New Zealand. The majority have to charge parents a fee in order to meet the difference between the costs of running a centre and the government funding that is available.

In the 1980s there was a resurgence of things Māori, including the renewal of the Māori language. Kōhanga Reo was initiated as a means of renewing the Reo (language) within families. It relied on older members of communities who still retained the language spending time with children so a new generation of children could learn (Royal Tangaere, 1997). This has sometimes led to tensions between the trust that administers Kōhanga and the Ministry of Education, whose focus is on early childhood education rather than family development. While the number of children attending Kōhanga is small, there are now as many of these centres as there are kindergartens.

More recently we are seeing the introduction of the term *child rights* into the discourse of early childhood. This year saw the introduction of 20 hours per week free early childhood education for 3- and 4-year-olds. Initially, this was only going to be available to community-based services rather than those that were privately owned. The main argument given for the expansion to privately based services was that a family should not be penalised for choosing a centre that is administered differently. Not all early childhood services have gone into the scheme, as the government was limiting the funds a service could get for each child place made available and a service could not charge a supplemental fee, except for minimal amounts to cover the provision of such things as meals. Thus some services would have had to accept a reduction in funding to join the scheme. Playcentres have not received additional funding for their 3- and 4-year-olds, as they were largely free to begin with. This service type is then felt to be unsupported in its attempt to improve service quality, as it is not being given access to a large pool of new early childhood funding. This creates pressure on other services to become more like full-day teacher-led services, and an unintended consequence of the policy may be an ongoing reduction in the diversity of services that can exist in the current policy environment.

The development of early childhood education has been very quick once the commitment was made to establish early childhood as the domain of education, rather than trying to separate out the services. The challenge has been to maintain diversity in spite of tensions rather than trying to eliminate those tensions. The new framework of legislation, funding, regulation, and rules could reduce the diversity in its attempt to promote the sector's development. The school system has been through its own changes, but not as quickly. Also, the system of schools in place retains a sense of consistency that means it is not as diverse as the early childhood sector. The sector has been able to prevent the pushdown of systems from school through to early childhood. The current strategy is about improving transition to school, but not by making the early childhood sector more like schools, so when new schools are built, consideration is given to making space available for early childhood services alongside rather than onsite. The sense of difference and diversity, and the idea that ECE is not about preparing children for school but providing for their current development, are central to ongoing policy development.

NOTE

1. *Te Reo* is the Māori term for "language," and *Tikanga* is the term for "customs." *Mokopuna* is a reference to children, who may also be called *Tamariki,* and *whānau* is the Māori term for "family," which includes the extended family.

REFERENCES

Carr, M. (2001). *Assessment in early childhood settings: Learning stories.* London: Paul Chapman.

Central Intelligence Agency. (2007, June 19). *CIA–The World Fact Book–New Zealand.* Retrieved July 14, 2007, from https://www.cia.gov/library/publications/the-world-factbook/geos/nz.html

Costa, A. L., & Kallick, B. (2000). *Discovering and exploring habits of mind* (A Developmental Series, Book 1). Alexandria, VA: Association for Supervision and Curriculum Development.

Gaffney, M. (2003). *An evaluation of Ministry of Education funded Early Childhood Education Professional Development Programmes.* Dunedin, NZ: Children's Issues Centre.

May, H. (1997). *The discovery of early childhood.* Wellington: New Zealand Council for Educational Research.

May, H. (2003). *School beginnings: A history of early years schooling—case study one: Missionary Infant Schools for Maori children 1830–1840s.* Wellington: Institute for Early Childhood Studies, Victoria University.

May, H. (2004). *School beginnings: A history of early years schooling—case study two: Dreams and realities for the youngest colonial settlers, 1840–50s.* Wellington: Institute for Early Childhood Studies, Victoria University.

Meade, A. (2002). Remembering: Knowing the moment cannot be repeated. *Childrenz Issues, 6*(2), 12–17.

Ministry of Education. (1993). *The New Zealand National Curriculum Framework.* Wellington: Learning Media.

Ministry of Education. (1996). *Te Whāriki. He Whāriki Mātauranga mö ngä Mokopuna o Aotearoa: Early childhood curriculum.* Wellington: Learning Media.

Ministry of Education. (2002). *Pathways to the future: Ngä Huarahi Arataki A 10-year strategic plan for early childhood education 2002–2012.* Wellington: Learning Media. Retrieved January 30, 2003, from http://www.minedu.govt.nz

Ministry of Education. (2003, May). *Schooling in New Zealand—A guide.* Retrieved July 5, 2005, from http://www.minedu.govt.nz

Ministry of Education. (2005). *Kei Tua o te Pae: Assessment for learning: Early childhood exemplars.* Wellington: Learning Media.

Ministry of Education. (2007a). *Statement of Intent: 2007–2012.* Wellington: Author.

Ministry of Education. (2007b). *Working in partnership: Information for new school trustees 2007–2010.* Wellington: Author.

New Zealand National Commission for UNESCO. (1952). *Compulsory education in New Zealand.* Wellington: Author.

Royal Tangaere, A. (1997). *Learning Maori together: Kohanga Reo and the home.* Wellington: New Zealand Council for Educational Research.

Smith, A. B., (2003, July 16). *Te Whāriki: Diversity or standardisation? Innovative aspects of the New Zealand early childhood curriculum.* Paper presented at Education in the Early Years: International developments and implications for Germany, Munich.

CHAPTER 7

Early Education in Sweden
Linking Preschool to School

INGE JOHANSSON

Sweden has a long tradition of combining care and education for young children in formal institutions. For the youngest children the main form is preschool. School starts when children are 7. In this chapter, I will give a short overview of the tradition of the preschool and the current reform effort to link preschool to school, and what these reforms have meant to both institutions. I will also put forward some questions that are on the agenda in the current national discussion.

The Swedish system offers preschool to the youngest children, ages 1 to 5. For 6-year-olds there is a special form called the preschool class. It aims to facilitate the transition from preschool to school but is formally a part of school. Compulsory school begins for 7-year-olds. For children in the preschool class and in the first years in school there is also afterschool day care, where most children go.

In this chapter the focus is on the preschool and the reform process there. The Swedish preschool has undergone significant changes during recent years. It has been defined as the first part of the nation's educational system. The first national preschool curriculum was established in 1998 (Utbildningsdepartementet [Ministry of Education and Science], 1998b), and the education of preschool teachers was changed in 2001. Parallel to this the compulsory school also has undergone reform (Utbildningsdepartementet, 1998a). The responsibility for the running of school was decentralized from the state to the local community level in 1991. A new curriculum for the schools, including the preschool and the afterschool day care (leisure-time center), was established in 1998. The education of schoolteachers was changed in 2001 in the same way as for preschool teachers, meaning that all teachers in preschool and the first 6 years of compulsory school have an education of the same length–3½ years. The first year of teacher education is the same for all. After that the students can choose the content of the next 2½ years of education depending on whether they prefer to become a teacher mainly in preschool, in the leisure-time center, or in compulsory school.

To understand and to analyze these reforms we need to learn from the tradition of the preschool in relation to school, family, and society.

THE SWEDISH SYSTEM AND THE PRESENT SITUATION

Preschool in Sweden is, as stated above, for children between 1 and 5 years old. Six-year-olds go to a specific school form called the preschool class (*förskoleklass* in Swedish). This is voluntary and includes 525 hours per year (normally 3 hours per day) and is often combined with a place in afterschool day care. More than 96% of 6-year-olds attend this service (National Agency of Education, 2005). The preschool is led by specially educated preschool teachers. Besides preschool there is also family day care, which means that children can be taken care of in another person's home. This child minder normally has no formal education for the work in the family day care. In this chapter the main interest is preschool, so family day care will not be discussed any further.

Sweden is, like Denmark and Finland, one of the countries in Europe that started to build up its preschool sector rather early, in the early 1970s. The aim was to support the family and especially the young mothers who wanted to engage in paid work outside the home. Preschool at that time was a part of the social service sector. This system has developed to the point where today a majority of children are in preschool by age 2. The proportions of children who have a place in a preschool or in family day care are seen in Table 7.1.

The relatively small proportion of the youngest children who attend preschool is due to the generous policy on parental leave in Sweden. Parental leave altogether is 18 months (the father must use at least two of them). This means that one of the parents stays home with the child until he or she reaches age 1. For those who can't do so (a very small proportion), more specialized solutions other than the regular preschool are found. The proportion of men taking advantage of the funded parental leave has increased rapidly during the last year. Today about 80% of fathers use at least a part of the paid parental leave.

TABLE 7.1. Percentage of Children Aged 1–5 Registered in Preschool Services, 2003

Age of child	Preschool	Family day care	Total
1 year	40	5	45
2 years	78	8	86
3 years	83	8	91
4 years	88	8	96
5 years	89	7	96
All	75	7	82

Source: The Ministry of Education and Science in Sweden

Another factor that has implications for quality is how many children there are in a preschool group. How the number of children has changed is illustrated in Table 7.2.

As we can see, the average number of children in the preschool group has increased during this period but has been relatively stable in recent years. For comparison, there are approximately 22 to 23 children in a typical school class during the first compulsory school years. For the youngest children in the preschool there is sometimes a special group for 1- to 3-year-olds. In these, the number of children in the group is lower and the child-staff ratio is lower compared to the average figures presented in Table 7.2.

Chronology

The main steps in the reform process linking preschool to school are summarized below.

July 1, 1996. Responsibility for preschool services and school-age child care is transferred to the Ministry of Education and Science.

January 1, 1998. National Agency for Education takes over supervisory responsibility for preschool services and school-age child care.

January 1, 1998. Preschool class is established as a special grade level of school.

July 1, 1998. Preschool acquires a curriculum (Lpfö 98, Utbildningsdepartementet, Ministry of Education and Science, 1998b).

July 1, 2001. Children of unemployed parents are entitled to attend preschool.

January 1, 2002. Maximum fees are introduced for preschool, family day care, and leisure-time centers.

TABLE **7.2. Average Number of Children in Preschool Group and the Staff-to-Child Ratio, 1990–2003**

Year	Children/group	Children/staff
1990	13.8	4.4
1992	15.7	4.8
1994	16.5	5.2
1996	16.9	5.5
1998	16.5	5.7
2001	17.5	5.3
2002	17.4	5.3
2003	17.2	5.4

Source: The Ministry of Education and Science in Sweden

January 1, 2002. Children of parents on parental leave are entitled to attend preschool.

January 1, 2003. Universal free preschool is introduced for children aged 4 and 5, for at least 525 hours per year.

Funding

The compulsory school and certain parts of preschool (as we see above) are funded by public taxes. For a place in the preschool and in a leisure-time center, parents have to pay a fee depending on their household income. However, there is a maximum fee. This means that no family must pay more than approximately 135 Euros per month for a full-time place for their child. There is also a reduction for the second and third child. The proportion of total expenditures on services for children below compulsory school age paid by parents was 11% in 2003. The total public expenditure on services for children in the same group and for school-age child care was 1.9% of GDP in 2002.

THE TRADITION OF THE SWEDISH PRESCHOOL

In the history of the Swedish preschool there are two philosophers who have been of significant importance to the development of the ideas that form the pedagogical content of the services. One is Robert Owen of England (1771–1858) and the other is Friedrich Froebel of Germany (1782–1852). Of the two Friedrich Froebel is the most influential on the pedagogical work in Swedish preschools. For Froebel, play was essential for the development of the child. Froebel created a place for children called *Kindergarten,* which was meant to be a setting for promoting the development of a free person. The word *garden* focuses on growing, not in the non-guided sense, but from conscious thriving. Besides play, the discovery of nature, thriving, and the bringing up of the child in the home are foundations for the work in kindergarten. We can still recognize such principles in our modern preschool as well as in the curriculum. Froebel also took initiatives to increase the awareness among women of his ideas of the "good garden" for small children. His message was that kindergarten should not be compensation for the home but a complement to it. This way of looking at the relationship between home and preschool is still articulated in the Swedish curriculum.

In 1836 the first infant school (for children under age 7) started in Sweden. That was 6 years earlier than the national act stating that all children had to go to school, which came in 1842. This means that the preschool and the school each developed their own specific tradition over a long period. From the 1930s, when the Social Democratic government begun building "the strong society" to support the family and children, until 1996, preschool was a part of the social welfare sector.

The Basic Philosophy

The hallmark of the pedagogical work in the preschool is the integration of care and education. Development of knowledge and caring relations based on good emotional quality go hand-in-hand. The tasks of the preschool are to stimulate the development of the whole child and be the first link in a chain of a universal educational system for the individual.

Current preschool pedagogy in Sweden is not dominated by just one theory or attitude but rather by the parallel development and application of different theories as the basis for practical pedagogical work (Johansson, 2004). Froebel and his view of the child as a flower to be cultivated are still present. Interaction theories are also highly influential, stressing relationships and their importance for development. The expansion of learning to include all senses and integration of intellect and emotion is surely here to stay. A good example of this kind of ideology is the pedagogical work inspired by Reggio Emilia. Another influential theory is the one developed by Maria Montessori. This theoretical direction stresses work based on the child's own natural development and the child's own instinct to be active (Pramling Samuelsson & Asplund Carlsson, 2003). All these ideas are present in the curriculum and are highly influential on the overall goal for the preschool.

The focus on quality and the importance of improving it are clearly stated in the official goals and the *Curriculum for the Preschool* (Government Bill 2004/05:11, 2004; Utbildningsdepartementet, 1998b).

The Preschool Curriculum

The word *curriculum* comes from Latin and basically means "running track," a certain defined distance you must go to reach a goal. In the basic pedagogical sense the concept of curriculum concerns the basic goals and directions for an education. A curriculum not only defines the goals but also states the guidelines for how to reach them.

A curriculum is always embedded in basic values, philosophical and theoretical views, and constructions of children's knowledge and learning typical to its country (Rosenthal, 2003). In this respect a curriculum is an important document for reproducing the main culture and visualizes the goals for the further development of the whole society. It also states what importance education has for such development. By tradition Swedish society has had and still has a trust in education to change society and to fulfill the political visions of a democratic society.

In 1996, as mentioned earlier, responsibilities for preschool activities and school-age child care were shifted from the Ministry of Health and Social Services to the Ministry of Education and Science. The provisions governing child care were transferred in 1998 from the Social Services Act to the School Act. In conjunction with this, the National Agency for Education assumed the responsibility for child care from the National Board of Health and Welfare.

During this period the age when children should start school was discussed. Traditionally children in Sweden start school when they are 7 years old. The reasons for this are still unclear. One thing that may have had an impact is that Sweden is a rather sparsely populated country where many people lived in small villages in the countryside until 100 years ago. This meant that many children had a long way to go to their school, and this, together with a cold climate, led to the comparatively high age for starting school. The recent interest in lowering the school starting age was, as I see it, precipitated by two main forces. One influential circumstance was that Sweden had become a member of the European Union, most of whose member countries had a school starting age of 6 (except Great Britain). The other reason was economic. Sweden had a significant economic recession in that period and a place in a school is cheaper than one in a preschool, so there is a lot of governmental money to be saved by "taking away" one year of preschool.

The possibility of changing the system to begin earlier (for example, when the child is 6) was investigated by a governmental committee. The result of this work can be seen as a compromise: Seven remains the age when compulsory schooling begins.

When the preschool formally became the first link in a coherent educational system, the logical step was to develop a national curriculum for it. Another government committee did this, and in 1998 the government established the new curriculum for 1- to 5-year-olds in preschool. The curriculum is based on a division of responsibility where the state determines the overall goals and guidelines for preschool and the municipalities take responsibility for implementation. In its structure the preschool curriculum is consistent with the other curricula for the school system. The curriculum will also provide a foundation for assessing quality when determining whether an individual preschool fulfills its stipulated requirements. The curriculum sets out the fundamental values for preschool and the tasks, goals, and guidelines for preschool activities.

The goals in the curriculum are just that: goals to be aimed at. They stipulate what the preschool should aim for in terms of the individual development and learning of the child. In preschool, individual child outcomes will not be formally assessed in terms of grades and evaluation. This is a difference between the preschool curriculum and compulsory school curricula.

Fundamental Principles of the Curriculum

In its structure the curriculum of the preschool is consistent with the other curricula for the school system. The aim is that the curricula should link with one another and take a common view of knowledge development and learning.

The structure of the curriculum means that the basis for the work in the preschool is fundamental values, meaning democracy. Five areas are identified where goals and guidelines are given. These are:

- Norms and values
- Development and learning
- Influence of the child
- Preschool and home
- Cooperation among the preschool class, the school, and the leisure-time center

The goals in "Norms and values" establish that the preschool should strive to ensure that each child develops:

- openness, respect, solidarity, and responsibility,
- the ability to take account of and empathize with the situation of others as well as a willingness to help others,
- the ability to discover, reflect on, and work out a position on different ethical dilemmas and fundamental questions of life in daily reality,
- an understanding that all persons have equal value independent of gender or social or ethnic background, and
- respect for all forms of life as well as care for the surrounding environment.

In the area "Development and learning" the preschool should try to ensure that children:

- develop their identity and feel secure in themselves,
- develop their curiosity and enjoyment at the same time as their ability to play and learn,
- develop self-autonomy and confidence in their own ability,
- feel a sense of participation in their own culture and develop a feeling and respect for other cultures,
- develop their ability to listen, narrate, reflect, and express their own views,

- develop their ability to function individually and in a group and to handle conflicts and understand rights and obligations as well as take responsibility for common rules,
- develop their motor skills, ability to coordinate, and awareness of their own body, as well as an understanding of the importance of maintaining their own health and well-being,
- acquire and be able to differentiate shades of meaning in concepts, see interconnections, and discover new ways of understanding the surrounding world,
- develop a rich and varied spoken language and the ability to communicate with others and to express their own thoughts,
- develop their vocabulary and concepts, the ability to play with words, an interest in the written language, and an understanding of symbols as well as their communicative functions,
- develop creative abilities and the ability to convey thoughts and experiences in many different forms of expression, such as play, pictures, song and music, dance, and drama,
- develop their ability to build, create, and design using different materials and techniques,
- develop the ability to discover and use mathematics in meaningful contexts and situations,
- develop their appreciation of the basic characteristics of the concept of number, measurement, and form, as well as the ability to orient themselves in time and space, and
- develop an understanding of their own involvement in the process of nature and in simple scientific phenomena, such as knowledge of plants and animals.

The goals that deal with the "Influence of the child" say that the preschool should try to ensure that children:

- develop the ability to express their thoughts and views and thus have the opportunity to influence their own situation,
- develop their ability to accept responsibility for their own actions and for the environment of the preschool, and
- develop the ability to understand and act in accordance with democratic principles by participating in different kinds of cooperation and decision making.

The goals in the area "Preschool and home" say that, for example, the preschool should supplement the home by creating the best possible preconditions for ensuring that each child's development is rich and varied. The preschool's work with children should thus take place in close and confidential cooperation with the home.

In the last area, "Cooperation among the preschool class, the school, and the leisure-time center," the curriculum says that in order to support the all-around development of children, the preschool should try to establish good working cooperation with both the school and the afterschool center in order to support the child's all-around development and learning for the future.

The activities of the preschool should be planned, implemented, assessed, and developed in relation to the goals in the curriculum. Attaining the goals of the curriculum requires a well-educated staff that is provided with the opportunity to enhance their competence and receive the support necessary for them to carry out their task professionally (Utbildningsdepartementet, 1998b, pp. 4–5). This stresses the importance of educated teachers working to improve quality in the preschool.

One of the main tasks for the preschool is to lay the foundation for life-long learning. The experiences and stimulation the child gets in the preschool setting influence both how he or she later judges other educational settings and the attitude toward learning. Therefore, the preschool should be enjoyable, secure, and rich in learning for all children. The connection to the family is clearly stated and says that children's development into responsible persons and members of society should be promoted in partnership with the home. In this respect the preschool should take account of the fact that children have different living environments and that they try to create context and meaning from their own experiences. The responsibility to fulfill this lies at the municipal level and mainly in the professional competence of the staff and leaders of the local preschool. This is supervised by the national education agency and guided by the goals in the curriculum.

National Acts to Develop and Maintain Quality Preschools

The reformed Educational Act (in preparation) concerns preschool. The government summarizes in a bill to the Swedish Riksdag steps taken in this new legislation in order to maintain and develop quality in the preschool (Government Bill 2004/05:11).

Preschool as a Special Grade of School. Preschool will be incorporated into the school system as a special grade of school with the same overall objectives as other forms of school. The primary purpose is to emphasize that the preschool is for the children's own sake and is the first stage in life-long learning. Preschool will still have the task of providing children with good educational activities.

Care, development, and learning will continue to form a cohesive whole, based on play and centered on the child.

Government Grants for Extra Staff. A special government grant will be provided to municipalities over a 3-year period to enable them to employ an extra 6,000 preschool teachers and other preschool staff. After this period the grant will become part of the general governmental grant to municipalities. The grant is intended to improve preschool staff-to-child ratios, with a view to reducing the number of children in each group so as to raise quality.

Preschool Management. A preschool must have a head teacher (*rektor*) in charge, who will coordinate educational activities within her or his area of responsibility. The head teacher is responsible for systematic quality enhancement and is to develop the preschool's activities in line with the objectives set out in the curriculum.

Preschool Staff. The staff and its knowledge and skills are important for quality. Research in the school and preschool sector has shown that teachers are the most important factor in the quality of the service (Gustafsson & Myrberg, 2002; Sheridan, 2001). Both preschool teachers and child care providers are needed in the preschool. This means that both staff with a formal pedagogical education as well as those with other qualifications have a role in the preschool. Formal qualifications will be introduced for preschool teachers. This will mean that every preschool must have qualified preschool teachers. The role of preschool teachers will be clarified so as to give them a special overall responsibility for ensuring that the goal-oriented educational activities advance children's development and learning. A Swedish teaching degree or equivalent qualification will be required to qualify as a preschool teacher.

Parents in Preschool—Cooperation and Influence. Enhanced cooperation is needed between homes and preschool. In addition to continuous exchanges in daily meetings and more structured activities for parents, staff and parents must engage in a dialogue about the child's development and learning at least once every 6 months.

Systematic Quality Enhancement in Preschool. It is important that preschool services develop systematic quality enhancement activities. The work should be documented to support the development of services. All forms of services, *public as well as private,* in the preschool system must report on their quality enhancement activities.

The content of these principles can very well also be applied to the goals and content of compulsory school.

RESULTS FROM RESEARCH AND
THE FIRST NATIONAL EVALUATION OF PRESCHOOL

In the last 10 years there has been a wide range of studies of the quality of preschool. Several of those have used the Early Childhood Environment Rating Scale (ECERS-R; Harms, Clifford, & Cryer, 2005). On the local level the type of evaluation method mostly used in preschool and school is probably self-evaluation. This approach can be more or less structured and is often qualitative. The quality of Swedish preschools is often conceived as high, even, and equal all over the country (Ministry of Education and Science, 1999). However, several evaluations with the ECERS show a variety within and between communities (Andersson, 1999; Kärrby & Giota, 1995; Sheridan, 1997). All of these studies show a similar pattern, leading to the conclusion that there is a great variation in quality in the Swedish preschool, both within and between communities. In her doctoral thesis Sheridan (2001) studied the development and assessment of quality from various perspectives. When the quality of preschool was evaluated by both the staff working in the service and by external evaluators, she found that the staff generally tended to assess the quality of their service higher than the external evaluators.

The results from this study show that evaluations that are expected to lead to change and development must be a combination of external and self-evaluations. Sheridan says that it is in the meeting between those evaluations that quality enhancement ensues. In another study in her thesis the children from a group of preschools, three with a low-quality rating on ECERS and three with a high rating, were asked about the content of their preschool. The results indicate that there is a difference between the children's experience of exercising influence depending on the level of quality in preschool. High-quality preschool units seemed to have a more open atmosphere, inviting children to participate and negotiate. The results from this study show that an evaluation of the quality of early childhood education must include the voices of children. The conclusion from these studies (Sheridan, 2001) is that the tradition of preschool is still strong. That pedagogical view is socially deeply rooted and focuses on child-initiated activities, the whole child, play, and creative activities as a way to learn, and on the belief that the role of the teacher is to foster children's social competence. The results imply that if the pedagogical quality in preschool is to be improved, then the activities and content have to be more learning-oriented. In this respect the role of the teacher becomes crucial.

In a meta-analysis of recent research, Haug (2003) concludes that there should be more focus on the quality of the pedagogical work in the preschool and its consequences, rather than on the quality of the structural processes. He also argues for tighter links between research and evaluation in order to identify more long-lasting and general knowledge about quality and how it develops in the preschool sector. This implies better cooperation between different sources in the formation of new knowledge and promoting understanding of the content of the work in the preschool sector.

PRESCHOOL IN TRANSITION

In 2004 the results from the first national evaluation of preschool were presented (National Agency of Education, 2004). The overall aim of the evaluation was to examine how preschool has developed after reform (the inclusion in the educational system and the new curriculum) and to study the importance of reform in its development.

In the evaluation three different substudies have been carried out: a meta-analysis of research about and evaluations of the preschool, published during the years 1998–2001; a questionnaire survey directed to the municipal heads of education in all municipalities; and case studies of a sample of 10 municipalities and 33 preschool units located in different kinds of catchment areas, where municipal heads of education, preschool heads, and preschool staff were interviewed. In connection with the case studies, different types of plans and other written documents were collected.

The evaluation shows that the curriculum has been received positively by administrators, heads of preschools, and preschool staff. This is unusual compared to the reception given to the curricula reforms in the schools. The fact that the preschool, which by tradition has a low status and no curriculum, has been incorporated into a new system that has higher status has led to a positive change for the professionals. The results also show that the curriculum has fulfilled many different functions, but has only had a marginal effect on municipal decisions concerning support structures and resources. The curriculum has been most important in terms of providing confirmation of the preschool's ways of working and raising its status, but it has also been of importance in providing support to staff in their pedagogical work. An important prerequisite for implementation of a reform—namely, that it have widespread support—was fulfilled in this case. The curriculum has had a psychological impact and has been taken seriously by all groups consulted in the evaluation.

In terms of organization and management, the evaluation shows that the reform efforts to bring about a closer linkage between preschool and school have had a major impact. Teachers and local program directors are expected to determine how best to implement the intentions of the curriculum. Many tools used in carrying out the task have been studied, such as how municipalities and preschools accomplish planning, pedagogical documentation, joint reflection, and evaluation and competence development. These are important in contributing to building up a common platform for the work of the staff, creating a shared understanding of the task and developing effective work teams. These tools are also crucial for the staff to be able to adapt the preschool to local conditions and to the needs and preconditions of their own groups of children.

The preschool's incorporation into a goal- and result-oriented educational system has had an impact on views concerning goal attainment in the preschool and how this can be measured and assessed. At the municipal level, the idea of goal setting has been well accepted, and attempts have been made in evaluations and quality reports to make preschool activities transparent and assess goal attainment. Formulating goals that are specific to preschool and evaluating these are not without problems. In the majority of municipalities, the preschool and school are treated jointly in the school plan and quality reporting. In documents, emphasis is put on what is regarded as shared in terms of their tasks and goals without discussing the problem that the preschool and the school also have different types of goals. This means that the boundary between goals to strive for and goals to attain becomes more ambiguous and less transparent. Sometimes, the consequence is that the goals of school become the norm even when assessing preschool.

To sum up, the evaluation shows that preschool is in a period of transition where an earlier tradition based on assessments of how the preschool is developing as a whole confronts new requirements to make results transparent and to more clearly assess goal attainment in relation to specific goals and goal areas. In this context, the assessment of the child's development more often becomes a starting point for evaluating the quality of the preschool.

The process of change initiated after the reform is in certain respects in line with the intentions of the curriculum. In many preschools, there is greater awareness of the task and how it can be implemented. There are also indications of greater flexibility in planning and use of premises, as well as greater effort to base work on the children's own initiative and interests, and enhance their involvement. Work on documentation has also become more common in the preschool in recent years. The view of competence development for those who work in the preschool has also changed from having been steered by individual inservice needs earlier. Today there is a tendency to give priority to competence development based on the needs of the preschool or the overall needs of the staff.

The evaluation shows that the child's individual development is increasingly focused on in the preschool, sometimes with school as a model. It is common that the individual child's development is mapped, observed, and documented. One example of this is that individual development plans have become increasingly common in preschool in recent years. In half of the municipalities studied, demands for individual development plans were imposed, and many preschools have also introduced such plans on their own initiative. The incorporation of preschool into the educational system appears to have been a starting point for such work, despite the fact that the curriculum for the preschool does not lay down any requirements for individual plans. According to documents issued by the ministry and the government, such requirements are only to be imposed on compulsory school.

Preschool's incorporation into the educational system has created benefits from a professional perspective in that the preschool gains higher status and increased legitimacy. This could be one explanation for the relatively great impact of the reform and the fact that it has received such positive acceptance. From a child's perspective, the benefits may be more uncertain, and dependent on the direction in which the preschool develops. The main reason for such a conclusion is that the National Agency for Education considers that excessive emphasis placed on formal learning at an early stage can have negative consequences and be in conflict with the overall goals of the curriculum.

CHALLENGES AND QUESTIONS FOR THE FUTURE

The reform of the Swedish educational system in general and preschool in particular can be seen as a radical effort to simultaneously reform the goals, structure, and content. This indicates, as I see it, two trends in the policy. One is to integrate preschool into the educational system, as the first part of a process of life-long learning. The other trend is to keep and develop preschool pedagogy and build on the preschool tradition and the goals and principles of the curriculum. A major challenge for the future will be to develop the content of the preschool in a way that responds to both the demand to make preschool a part of school and the desire to maintain the emphasis on individual child needs and relationships with families.

One crucial element of the success of that effort is the new teacher education. Teachers are trained for a wider role than just to work in one specific form of service. Teachers with the same basic training can work in preschool as well as in the preschool class for 6-year-olds and the first grades of the compulsory school. This can be expected to lead to increased integration, especially when most of the work is done in teams of teachers with different specializations (preschool, the preschool class, and compulsory school). The interesting question here is, how will preschool teachers and their practices be influenced? This is one crucial question for future research and policy evaluations.

Linking preschool to school is not only a matter of organization; it is confronting two cultures with each other. These two cultures have different traditions and different ways of seeing the child and the outcome of their work. In such a heterogeneous system the transitions become essential. This means vertical (preschool to school) as well as horizontal transitions (for example, between school and leisure-time center).

Two U.S. researchers (Kagan & Neuman, 1998) have analyzed the content of the transition concept in a metastudy of 3 decades of transition research. They found three main interpretations of the concept. One regards transition as one-time activities undertaken by children, families, and programs at the end of the year. Another regards transition as an ongoing effort to create linkages between children's natural and support environments (i.e., linking families to programs, children to their communities). A third group regards transition as the manifestation of the developmental principle of continuity (e.g., creating pedagogical, curricular, and/or disciplinary approaches that transcend, and continue between, programs). From this, transitions are defined as the continuity of experiences that children have between periods and between spheres of their lives (Zigler & Kagan, 1982).

Transitions affect children in many ways, their own development as well as their relations to their sociocultural context from one time to another. The preschool-to-school transition involves rapid and often unanticipated change within a compressed period of time (Margetts, 2000). To study this process of transition and facilitate it to be as smooth as possible are crucial tasks for future research and developmental work.

Perhaps the most significant change in modern childhood is that, increasingly, children are living a greater part of their early childhood in out-of-home settings, and often in multiple settings with multiple caregivers (Neuman, 2002). While transitions can be viewed as learning opportunities for children, there are risks that children who experience difficult transitions will have difficulties adjusting to school and making friends, and will face emotional and health problems. These risks are especially significant for children with special needs and diverse cultural backgrounds.

Sweden is, like many other countries, becoming a multicultural and multiethnic society. A great challenge for the future is to gain knowledge of how this affects the pedagogical work in the preschool, school, and afterschool day care. As I see it, a main task for the education of teachers is to form a professional competence that can use the curriculum as well as the educational arena to maintain and further develop a foundation for a democratic society.

REFERENCES

Andersson, M. (1999). *The Early Childhood Environmental Rating Scale (ECERS) as a tool in evaluating and improving quality in preschools* (Studies in Educational Sciences 19). Stockholm: Institute of Education Press.

Government Bill 2004/05:11. (2004). *Quality in preschool.* Stockholm: Ministry of Education and Science.

Gustafsson, J-E., & Myrberg, E. (2002). *Ekonomiska resursers betydelse för pedagogiska resultat. En kunskapsöversikt* [The impact of economical resources on educational results]. Stockholm: Liber.

Harms, T., Clifford, R., & Cryer, D. (2005). *The Early Childhood Environment Rating Scale* (Rev. Ed.) *[ECERS-R]*. New York: Teachers College Press.

Haug, P. (2003). *Om kvalitet i förskolan* [On quality in preschool]. *Forskning om och utvärderingar av förskolan 1998–2001. Forskning i fokus nr 8* [Research and evaluation of preschool. Research on focus no. 8]. Stockholm: National Agency for Education.

Johansson, I. (2004, June). *The Swedish model of early childhood education: Theoretical framework and policy approaches.* Keynote address presented at the Quality Education in the Early Years International Conference, University of Bolzano, Italy.

Kagan, S. L., & Neuman, M. J. (1998). Lessons from three decades of transition research. *The Elementary School Journal, 98*(4), 365–380.

Kärrby, G., & Giota, J. (1995). Parental conceptions of quality in day care centres in relation to quality measured by the ECERS. *Early Childhood Development and Care, 104,* 1–22.

Margetts, K. (2000). Indicators of children's adjustment to the first year of schooling. *Journal of Australian Research in Early Childhood Education, 7*(1), 20–30.

Ministry of Education and Science. (1999). *OECD country note: Early childhood education and care policy in Sweden.* Stockholm: Utbildningsdepartementet.

National Agency of Education. (2004). *Preschool in transition: A national evaluation of the Swedish preschool.* (Summary of report 239). Stockholm: Skolverket.

National Agency of Education. (2005). *Barn, elever och personal–riksnivå* [Children, pupils and staff–the national level]. (Rapport 260). Stockholm: Skolverket.

Neuman, M. J. (2002). The wider context: An international overview of transition issues. In H. Fabian & A.-W. Dunlop (Eds.), *Transitions in the early years* (pp. 8–22). London: RoutledgeFalmer.

Pramling Samuelsson, I., & Asplund Carlsson, M. (2003). *Det lekande lärande barnet–I en utvecklingspedagogisk teori* [The playing learning child–in a developmental-pedagogical theory]. Stockholm: Liber.

Rosenthal, M. (2003). Quality in early childhood education and care. A cultural context. *European Early Childhood Education Research Journal, 11*(2), 101–116.

Sheridan, S. (1997). *Kvalitetsbedömningarmed The Early Childhood Environmental Rating Scale: En jämförelse mellan en extern utvärderas och förskolepersonals bedömning med ECERS* [Evaluation of quality with the Early Childhood Environmental Rating Scale: A comparison between exteral evaluations and preschool teachers' self-evaluations of quality with the ECERS]. Göteborg: Department of Education, Gothenburg University.

Sheridan, S. (2001). *Pedagogical quality in preschool.* Göteborg: Acta Universitatis Gothoburgensis.

Utbildningsdepartementet, Ministry of Education and Science. (1998a). *Curriculum for the compulsory school system, the preschool class and leisure-time centre (LPO94).* Stockholm: Fritzes.

Utbildningsdepartementet, Ministry of Education and Science. (1998b). *Curriculum for the preschool (LPfö98).* Stockholm: Fritzes.

Zigler, E., & Kagan, S. L. (1982). Child development knowledge and educational practice. In A. Liberman & M. McLaughlin (Eds.), *Policy making in education: Eighty-first yearbook of the National Society for the Study of Education* (pp. 80–104). Chicago: University of Chicago Press.

CHAPTER 8

Learning from One Another

RICHARD M. CLIFFORD

GISELE M. CRAWFORD

The authors of the preceding chapters gathered in Chapel Hill, North Carolina, with a small group of educators, scholars, and national leaders to discuss education for children from age 3 through 8 in our countries. We shared information about the various services offered to children, and how they are operated, financed, governed, staffed, and evaluated. We also asked how and why specific decisions had been made. Are early childhood services under the auspice of education or social service agencies, and why? What is the involvement of the private sector? How much do parents pay for programs for 3- and 4-year-olds, and for whom are these programs provided free of charge? At the root of these questions are more fundamental issues that every society must grapple with. What do we really mean by "school"? When does school begin? What is the content of school, what does school look like, and what is its purpose? Are early care and education programs defined by school, or do they define themselves? What do we expect of children, and who expects it? What role does school play between the family and the larger society? What is the balance between preservation of the best of what we have now and innovation–a problem that German philosophers in education were thinking about 400 years ago? This chapter draws on that discussion and the preceding chapters to compare and contrast the challenges faced by the different countries, their goals for children in this age group, and the various approaches to achieving those goals.

A STRUCTURAL COMPARISON

Relative Roles of Different Levels of Government and Different Agencies

Like the United States, all of these other countries have moved toward a greater role for government in providing education for children younger than primary school age. Some countries started this move to serve younger children before the United States did, and serve larger segments of the population in their early education programs. Each, in its own way, tries to integrate early childhood education into its larger system of government-supported services. In this section we summarize briefly the way early childhood education services are made a part of those systems.

France. The central government of France finances and oversees the école maternelle just as it does the higher levels of French schooling. The Ministry of Education sets the curriculum, and teachers are recruited by the French state. Local authorities are responsible for transportation, the upkeep and equipping of buildings, and the hiring of school helpers, the care staff who are in charge of before- and afterschool care centers, and the assistant teachers. Overall there is a high degree of integration into the education system and a strong central government role in policy and operation of programs. Financing is primarily by the national government, with some sliding-scale payments made for école maternelle by the parents.

Germany. In each German state, the Ministry of Education is responsible for all areas of compulsory school, which begins when children are about 6 years old. In general, elementary and secondary education is provided in public buildings. Construction and maintenance of the buildings is financed by the community (and sometimes by the state level, too), whereas the teachers are paid directly by the states. Private schools are very rare in Germany and quite expensive. Financing for the operation of institutions for early childhood care and education "comes from four sources: the respective agency . . . , community subsidies, state subsidies, and parental contributions" (Chapter 4, p. 57).

Kindergarten[1] is considered part of a child's education but is operated and governed in conjunction with youth and social welfare programs. Federal involvement largely consists of enacting legislation (*Kinder- und Jugendhilfegesetz*, Law on Child and Youth Welfare) and of formulating proposals, distributing information, and developing model projects. In 1996, the federal law on child and youth welfare established a right to kindergarten for all children starting at age 3 up to the start of compulsory education, with financing from state resources and small parental payments.

The establishment and operation of kindergartens and programs for younger children and afterschool care are regulated primarily at the state level. "Kindergartens are overseen in about half of the 16 states by the ministry of education and in the others by the ministry of youth and social welfare. In several of the states, there has been a shift from the ministry of youth and social welfare to the ministry of education in recent years, which is at least partly connected to the discussion to put more emphasis on cognitive stimulation and school preparation in Kindergarten" (Chapter 4, p. 57). So, in Germany, the national and state levels share responsibility, and at the state level there is a trend toward a greater role for education ministries.

Japan. From ages 3 to 6, children may be in kindergartens or nursery centers, which are overseen by different agencies. The kindergarten is under the authority of a department of the national Ministry of Education, Culture, Sports, Science and Technology, and the nursery center is under the authority of a department of the national Ministry of Health, Labor, and Welfare. The two agencies are trying to coordinate more closely and are sharing a building, but there are barriers to blending the two systems. The salary systems for kindergarten and nursery teachers are different. These agencies both provide separate inservice training, of similar quality.

The 6 years of elementary school and 3 years of junior high school are compulsory, and are provided free at public schools. The regulated national curriculum is applied to both public and private elementary schools.

The elementary school is monitored by each level of government: central, prefectural, and municipal. Each prefecture and municipality has its own Board of Education, which monitors the elementary school directly. At the central government level the Elementary and Secondary Education Bureau is responsible for establishing (1) curriculum standards in elementary schools as well as other schools, including the kindergarten; (2) the free provision and authorization of textbooks; (3) a system for local education; and (4) legal standards for class size, staffing numbers for schools, and the payment of school staff.

The educational system was developed quickly after World War II, so it made sense for the national government to be heavily involved. After 60 years this centralization is relaxing, with greater responsibility at the prefecture and municipal level. In the early childhood area, Japan, like Germany, has a split, with the education and social welfare ministries each having significant roles.

The regulated kindergarten and the certified nursery center are both subsidized by national and local governments through a grants system. Parents also contribute financially to both kindergarten and nursery centers.

New Zealand. The central government administers the school system through the Ministry of Education. "This ministry has the overall responsibility for formal early childhood education (ECE), compulsory education, and tertiary education" (Chapter 6, pp. 83–84). While the national government funds and licenses early childhood programs, they are operated by a variety of private and local government providers. To receive government funding the program must adhere to the educational requirements specified in the Ministry of Education rules called Desirable Objectives and Practices. Parents also pay fees, depending on the type of program and the number of hours of participation desired. When children turn 5 they begin attending state-sponsored schools, which in New Zealand are managed by their own Boards of Trustees. The costs of the preschool programs are supported by the central government and some parent fees.

Sweden. In 1996–98 the national Ministry of Education assumed oversight of programs for children starting at age 1. During this shift, Sweden has gone from being very centralized to less centralized. Giving more emphasis to local democratic processes. At the same time, the move of early childhood education into the educational system has had the intended integrative effect. Preschool teachers now have a higher standing, preschool is seen as the first part of a life-long learning process, and curricula for preschool and school are now linked.

United States. Most parents pay for early care and education for their children prior to kindergarten. However, a significant number of families receive some sort of government support to cover all or a portion of these costs. At the federal level, the U.S. Department of Health and Human Services funds the Head Start preschool program for disadvantaged children, as well as funding the major share of child care subsidy payments for low-income families. The U.S. Department of Education partially funds supplemental payments for services for children with disabilities (Individuals with Disabilities Education Act, IDEA) and also provides significant funding for children viewed at risk of poor educational performance through the No Child Left Behind Act. At the state level, human services departments provide child care–related funds. States increasingly are funding pre-kindergarten programs primarily for children in the year before they enter public kindergarten at about age 5 (a number of states also provide pre-K for some 3-year-olds, although the vast majority of children in pre-K are 4) through the educational system. Public school for children age 5 to 18 is provided free through a combination of state and local funding (more than 90% of total costs), supplemented by targeted federal funds.

Setting Standards

One of the key means of governing and guiding programs is through the process of setting standards.

France. Overall standards for the école maternelle are set by the national Ministry of Education. Standards for teacher training, class size, and curricula and the system of cycles to improve transitions and learning across years of schools have been put into place. Expectations for what children learn in école maternelle are very precise and are set by the Ministry of Education. In the first year of elementary school there is an assessment. The evaluation takes into account skills in language, math, science, and social competency, but does not address how these skills are to be achieved.

Ministry of Education inspectors, located all over France, are responsible for monitoring schoolteachers at all levels. The same inspectors assess both écoles maternelles and elementary schools. Care centers that offer extended day care have been required since 2002 to have a pedagogical program.

Germany. There are no national quality standards for Kindergarten in Germany, because nationally it does not belong to the field of education—it has belonged to social welfare since 1920. There is a great degree of freedom for providers in terms of the environments and programs they offer. There is some discussion about using an instrument like the *Early Childhood Environment Rating Scale–Revised* (ECERS-R; Harms, Clifford, & Cryer, 2005) to measure quality, but the field of early childhood is not supportive of this movement. There are regulations governing health and safety, and programs generally meet high standards in these areas compared to other countries.

States all have state educational plans intended as guidelines for early childhood practice. Education plans are required to allow for local differences in implementation, and they do not require external evaluation. It is unknown how well the plans are realized in practice. None of these educational plans includes standards for child outcomes, which are strongly rejected by the field.

Japan. The national government subsidizes early childhood programs in Japan, but in the past has not collected data on quality. Efforts to assess the quality of these environments have been initiated. There are national standards for the certified nursery centers, but while there is a minimum standard that is met, these programs can look different from one another. A major new initiative, the Angel Plan, was enacted into law in 1996 and has strengthened the role of the national government and provided new financing of child care services. But the historically weak regulation of private child care persists to this day. Kindergartens also abide by a set of national standards, which certified nursery centers may also abide by if they choose to. There isn't much difference detected between children who enter primary school from the two different institutions.

New Zealand. The central government provides oversight of both early childhood centers and schools. There are 3,500 licensed centres, all of which have charters from the central government in order to get government money. "It is the responsibility of the Education Review Office to ensure that each school is meeting expectations around a board's legal responsibilities. Each school and early childhood service is inspected every 3 years, with reports made publicly available" (Chapter 6, p. 85).

Sweden. As the Swedish preschool has been redefined as the first part of the nation's educational system, this shift has brought about significant changes. The first national preschool curriculum was established in 1998, and the National Agency for Education took over supervisory responsibility for preschool services and school-age child care. This move is seen as quite positive, moving child care into the mainstream of education while retaining its special child-centered character. The decision to retain age 7 as the start of compulsory schooling was intentional, as an effort to preserve childhood and the special nature of settings that serve young children.

United States. Early childhood programs that receive federal Head Start funding must meet standards set by the Administration for Children, Youth and Families of the federal Department of Health and Human Services. Federal funding for children with disabilities carries specific criteria for programs as well. State pre-kindergarten programs have their own standards, and states also license child care providers, who must meet licensing standards. Child care centers and other early childhood providers can also opt to meet voluntary standards—for example, through accreditation by the National Association for the Education of Young Children.

Public elementary schools must meet standards set by their state education department, may choose to meet regional accrediting standards, and must also meet standards set by the federal No Child Left Behind Act if they wish to receive federal education funds.

Operating Programs

The countries examined in this book have made various decisions about the roles of various agencies in operating education programs. The greatest differences are in the provision of services for children prior to 1st grade. All countries provide publicly financed and operated schools beginning by about age 6. France has gone the furthest in centralizing formal schooling for young children, now serving children as young as age 2 in communities considered to have special priority. At the opposite end of the spectrum is New Zealand, which relies almost totally on community organizations and local government to operate educational programs for children under age 5.

France. The central government oversees the école maternelles just as it governs elementary and secondary school. Local authorities are responsible for maintaining and equipping the buildings. Typically écoles maternelles and elementary schools exist in separate buildings, though there are about 150 places in rural and mountain areas where they are in the same building. In France the écoles maternelles operate on the same school year schedule as primary school, with a 6-hour day. There are care centers open from 7:00 a.m. to 6:30 p.m. for parents who work. Some of these care centers are provided by the municipalities.

Germany. In Germany independent organization such as churches and social service or other philanthropic organizations operate Kindergartens, as do public authorities like the municipalities. They determine their own educational philosophies and goals, employ and supervise personnel, and are responsible for inservice professional development. "They also provide the buildings, which are not connected to the buildings for compulsory schooling" (Chapter 4, p. 57).

The KiDZ program is innovative in having a Kindergarten and elementary teacher work together, which is made possible through collaboration between the ministries that govern each system. The goal is for teachers to interact differently with children and work on both cognitive skills and active engagement in music, movement, language, early literacy, numeracy, and science.

Japan. "About 20% of kindergartens are run by local governments, and the rest are private" (Chapter 5, p. 69). Kindergartens are for 3- to 6-year-olds, and the mothers of kindergarten children often do not work outside the home. In Japan certified nursery schools serve children from birth to age 6. "For the last several years in some cities, privatization of public nursery centers has increased, and private nursery centers have been encouraged to accept infants and toddlers and to offer extended-hours service. Also, the government encourages nursery centers to accept children 11 hours or more per day" (Chapter 5, p. 74). A good nursery center and a good kindergarten are expected to provide similar experiences for children.

Extended day care for elementary children whose parents work is provided by private prep schools that provide extra education for children.

The cost of these early childhood programs is shared by the government and parents. Exact distribution of the costs is complicated by the fact that some payments are direct and others are more indirect and difficult to estimate.

New Zealand. A diverse range of early childhood settings have been created by families and communities in New Zealand. The national government strives to support these providers in a way that permits variation. Schools (and the early childhood Correspondence School) are state-owned and -run.

Sweden. In Sweden "the responsibility for the running of school was decentralized from the state to the local community level in 1991" (Chapter 7, p. 95). The preschool class for 6-year-olds is normally located in the school building. Services for children ages 1 to 5 could be connected to school, but will more likely be in an independent building outside the school. The municipalities actually operate most preschools. There might be mixed-age groups or single-age groups. The same head teacher interacts with the different groups. In the big cities there is a larger proportion of private providers.

Five or six percent of Swedish children are in family child care. In smaller villages the percentage could be higher. Parents may choose this because they have unusual work hours, or they feel the preschool group is too big.

United States. Early childhood programs for children from birth to age 5 are operated by private for-profit and nonprofit companies, school districts, and other local and county government agencies. Family child care is also common, with an individual providing care in a home setting for up to five or six children of mixed ages, and sometimes for more children with a second adult helping out. The mix of providers is quite diverse. They are generally regulated by state and local governments, but the level of regulation varies widely by state and by the type of provider, with full-day, center-based settings generally more heavily regulated and with family child care and center-based programs operated by religious organizations less regulated. By the end of children's first year of life, more than half of their mothers are in the paid workforce. Thus care and education by someone other than parents begins quite early in the United States.

A large majority of children are in public schools beginning at about age 5. The first year of formal school is known as kindergarten and was instituted as a transition to the school year. (Note that the term *Kindergarten* originated in Germany, where the term is still used for programs for children ages 3 through 5, as described earlier in this section.) Some 14% of children between 5 and about 18 attend private schools or are home-schooled by their parents (NCES, 2004). In the past decade state pre-kindergarten programs have been instituted or greatly expanded, now serving some 25% of the total population of children in the year prior to their eligibility for kindergarten (thus most of the children are 4). About half of these children are served in public school buildings, with the other half served in private programs, including Head Start programs and child care centers that agree to provide a class that meets the state pre-kindergarten standards.

Establishing Curricula

Inge Johansson describes curriculum as defining the goals of education and outlining the guidelines for achieving those goals. Governments often use the establishment of a curriculum as a major tool in influencing the delivery of services to young children.

France. The 1986 national curriculum states that "the école maternelle is a school" (Chapter 3, p. 41), clearly emphasizing the educational imperative. The 2002 edition structures children's learning around five domains of activities: oral language and an introduction to reading and writing; learning how to live together; expressing emotions and thoughts with one's body; discovering the world; and imagining, feeling, and creating. The project idea is a fundamental approach of the curriculum, and language must be a part of all projects, keeping language at the heart of learning.

Germany. State laws have dealt with general early childhood goals, but the agencies that operate the programs have had a great deal of autonomy to decide on their own educational philosophies, goals, and methods. However, in recent years states have begun developing educational plans for the early childhood care and education field, especially for Kindergarten. "These educational plans can be—at least partly—considered state curricula" (Chapter 4, p. 61).

In Germany until a few years ago letters and numbers were forbidden to be taught in Kindergarten. This changed after Germany's results in the Programme for International Student Assessment (PISA) study did not compare well against many other countries. Early childhood advocates would say that Kindergartens have a play-rich environment and school is sterile, but schools now have more flexibility—there are pictures on the walls and tables instead of desks. There are mixed-age groups in Kindergarten with two or three staff, while in elementary schools each class has one age group and one teacher.

Japan. In Japan the regulated national Course of Study applies to both public and private elementary schools, and is the basis for authorization of textbooks. The Elementary and Secondary Education Bureau also sets curriculum standards for the kindergarten, and nursery centers may follow these standards if they choose, in addition to meeting the national standards set by the Ministry of Health, Labor, and Welfare.

New Zealand. The New Zealand Ministry of Education provides a curriculum framework for schools, and "the development of the early childhood curriculum *Te Whāriki* . . . was a key feature of the 1990s early childhood policy" (Chapter 6, p. 87). The emphasis is on learning, not on teaching. The curriculum does not specify practices for adults but rather outcomes for children, and has at times been criticized for not supporting adults in articulating their practices, but the intention is to support the many different early childhood settings to take their own approaches.

There is a national curriculum for compulsory schooling. Private schools are not required to teach the curriculum but "are still visited by the Education

Review Office to ensure that legislative requirements are met and a programme of education is provided" (Chapter 6, p. 85).

Sweden. The first national preschool curriculum was established in 1998 by the national Ministry of Education and Science with curriculum principles that relate to all the ages of preschool. The same ministry establishes curricula for compulsory school and for afterschool care in the leisure-time centers.

United States. Child care centers typically choose their own curriculum, though accrediting bodies or state licensing agencies may restrict the choices. Similarly, state pre-kindergarten programs may require providers to select from a list of approved curricula. Head Start has extensive standards that in some ways may been seen as determining the curriculum, although individual Head Start agencies have authority to adopt the actual curriculum used. State departments of education typically publish a course of study for public schools to follow, and local districts make curriculum choices. However, state education agencies and affiliated groups often adopt one or more textbooks that local districts must choose from for use in public schools, thus in essence setting curricular choices for the schools.

Teacher Preparation

France. Teachers are educated at University Institutes (IUFM) and recruited by the French government. Their preparation lasts 2 years. The first year there is no distinction in the coursework for students whether they plan to teach in the école maternelle or in the elementary school. Students then spend a year preparing for an exam for teaching in either the école maternelle or elementary school. Teacher preparation emphasizes teaching methods for teaching French language and literacy, math, science, and physical education. There is some interest in including more sociology and psychology in teacher preparation coursework.

Germany. In Germany, elementary school teachers are educated at universities. Kindergarten teachers are not even educated at technical colleges, but at Category 5 institutions, which are at a lower level than technical college training. There is now debate that this should be increased at least to technical college, at least for directors. Advocates are pushing for programs to at least have the flexibility to hire a university-trained teacher for Kindergarten if they choose to.

Japan. In Japan, teachers are required to have at least a 2-year degree from a junior college or a university degree. Kindergarten teachers must have at least a 2-year degree as well, and "are required to have relevant teacher certifications awarded by prefectural boards of education as provided for by the Education Personnel Certification Law" (Chapter 5, p. 71). To be qualified as a nursery worker, it is necessary to complete a 2-year course at a university or college or to pass an examination offered by prefectural governments. "Qualified nursery workers often also have kindergarten teacher certificates" (Chapter 5, p. 74).

New Zealand. New Zealand is implementing a 10-year plan of education reform that promotes the goal of all early childhood teachers having at least a 3-year diploma and being registered in the same way that schoolteachers are. The challenge will be to find enough qualified teachers to fill the slots. Primary teachers have a 3-year degree, which can prepare a teacher for early childhood, primary, or secondary training. A degree has more of a research component, whereas a diploma is more practice-based. Degree teachers used to have more potential for raises in salary. There is now parity for kindergarten and primary teachers.

Sweden. Since 2001 all teachers in preschool and the first 6 years of compulsory school must have 3.5 years of education. "The first year of teacher education is the same for all" (Chapter 7, p. 95).

United States. Requirements for early childhood teacher preparation vary from state to state and from program to program. Many state pre-kindergarten programs require a bachelor's degree for lead teachers, but some states have no education requirement for child care teachers. Many child care teachers have a Child Development Associate (CDA) credential (roughly equivalent to 1 year of education), or a 2-year degree. Head Start has set goals for increasing professional preparation of teachers. NAEYC accreditation and some state licensing systems build in incentives for specific levels of teacher education, and many states and communities offer support to early childhood teachers seeking a higher degree. While incentives are in place to raise teacher qualifications, most teachers in preschool settings in the United States do not have a 4-year degree, and many have less than a year of postsecondary education.

Elementary school teachers are required to have at least a 4-year degree and certification by their state. Types of certification vary from state to state. For example, teachers may be certified to teach kindergarten through 5th grade, birth through kindergarten, pre-kindergarten through 3rd grade, and so on. Teachers may also receive certification in specific areas such as special education, music, or English as a second language. In general these certificates require a 4-year degree from an accredited institution of higher education.

DELIVERING EARLY EDUCATION SERVICES

Diverse Delivery Systems

In all six of the countries profiled, most children attend government-sponsored elementary schools starting between age 5 and age 7, with various arrangements for extended-day and extended-year care. Prior to elementary school, however, the delivery systems for education vary. In France the écoles maternelles are under the auspice of the central government in the same way that elementary schools are, and they are available throughout the country to all children beginning at age 3 and for even younger children in areas deemed to have a high need for support. The other four countries bear more similarity to the United States in having a history of a mixture of different private and public providers and different government agencies providing and overseeing these programs. All are moving toward greater coordination of early childhood services, and are taking somewhat different approaches to this task.

Germany. The German early childhood sector bears some similarities to the United States—the influence of individual states, the financing system being primarily at the state and local level, and a substantial amount of autonomy at the individual agency and programs level. Traditionally there has been a strict separation between Kindergarten and school, and Kindergartens have been operated by two major entities. The municipal agencies operate about half of Kindergartens, with religiously affiliated programs operating the remainder. These Kindergarten and school worlds are beginning to collide, with social welfare and education agencies fighting to control Kindergarten. The KiDZ initiative is an effort to work with both education and welfare agencies, but the realities of differential training of teachers in Kindergartens and in schools make implementation of this model using both Kindergarten- and elementary-trained teachers in the same class problematic. There is discussion of changing the education of Kindergarten teachers to better equip them to implement the KiDZ curriculum on their own.

Japan. Prior to formal school entry children may attend kindergartens (which are under the authority of the education ministry) or nurseries (which are under the authority of the health, labor, and welfare ministry). Seventy-nine percent of kindergartens are private, with an additional 20% provided by municipalities. Nurseries, providing what in the United States would be considered child care, are also prevalent in Japan. Privatization of public nursery centers is increasing, and there is a large group of uncertified private nurseries as well. While the Ministry of Health and Welfare has been striving to increase the supply of child care, both the education and health ministries are seeking avenues to build greater cohesion between the systems.

New Zealand. New Zealand is implementing a 10-year plan called *Pathways to the Future–2002–2012* to improve the quality of early childhood education services, to increase participation in those services, and to promote collaborative relationships. "One of the aims of the plan is to provide a system that maintains and supports the diverse range of services currently available to parents and families" (Chapter 6, p. 86), including education and care centres, home-based services, kindergartens, Kōhanga Reo (Māori language and customs), license-exempt play groups, parent support, and development programmes, playcentres, and Correspondence School early childhood services. These programs provide options for parents ranging from a few hours per week to full-day care, for children from birth to school age. They may be privately owned, non-profit-making, community-based services; operated as an adjunct to the main purpose of a business or organization (e.g., a crèche at a university or polytechnic); home-based caregivers; community-based groups of parents and children; or collectives supervised and managed by parents for children up to age 5.

Sweden. Swedish children age 6 and younger can attend preschool 3 hours a day for 170 days a year, with a focus on instruction. After lunch, those children can go to the leisure-time center, which provides full-time child care outside the home. As described above, preschool was originally a part of the social service sector, and is now under the auspice of the education sector and guided by a national curriculum. While Sweden does not have the diversity of provider organizations seen in New Zealand and the United States, there was a conscious decision to keep preschool in community settings separate from elementary school, even as preschool was brought into the purview of education.

Educators are committed to responding to both the demand for making preschool the first part of school and the desire to maintain the emphasis on individual child needs and relationships with families. The National Agency for Education has taken the position that excessive emphasis placed on formal learning at an early stage can have negative consequences and that this results in a conflict with the overall goals of the education system.

United States. The early childhood situation in the United States has been described as "parallel play" (Clifford, Cochran, & Kagan, 2003). In this country a variety of different providers, both public and private, are intimately involved in the delivery of services. These providers include

- State and locally funded pre-kindergarten programs primarily for 4-year-olds
- Head Start agencies embedded in a combination of private nonprofit and public agencies, including substantial participation by public

schools. Often Head Start agencies participate in the state pre-kindergarten in their respective states and school districts.
- Private for-profit and nonprofit organizations providing child care services, some of which are also tied into state pre-kindergarten programs
- Private, nonprofit, and public organizations providing services specifically to young children with special needs
- Independent preschool and nursery school programs, some of which are nonprofit and some for-profit

These programs are supervised by a complex set of local, state, and federal agencies, including both educational and health and human services agencies.

Transition for Children and Families among Settings

The transition to kindergarten is a major issue in early education in the United States. Educators, advocates, and political leaders debate about how to prepare children for school. In Chapter 1 we discuss the movement to focus on the readiness of schools to receive all children. Whether there should be greater alignment and coordination between early childhood settings and schools, and if so, how best to achieve those goals, is an issue each country has approached differently.

France. France has a systematic method for the transition between the various levels of school. The educational trajectory is divided into educational cycles that cross the normal school transitions. For instance, Cycle 2 includes the last year of école maternelle and the first 2 years of elementary school. A teacher's workday permits time outside the classroom for preparation and for meetings. One important meeting is for teachers working together within a cycle. In Cycle 2, teachers from the école maternelle work with teachers from the elementary school into which the école maternelle feeds in order to have a common project approach. They also talk about children who have difficulties. Of course, the success of the cycle varies from school to school. This work is most effective when teachers work together for a long time.

Elementary school is quite different from the école maternelle. Play is important at écoles maternelles, and this is reflected in the environment. Children do spend time in écoles maternelles as a group, to hear stories and to sing, but elementary school classrooms have rows of desks and, overall, a much more formal educational environment. The cycles provide an effective mechanism for bridging these settings.

Germany. In Germany in the 1970s there were school entrance classes to help children make the transition from the various Kindergarten settings to school. After these classes were discontinued, there was wide agreement that there should be more cooperation between the two settings, such as visiting, exchanging teachers for seminars, and parent meetings. In Chapter 4, Rossbach reported that three separate studies all found that cooperation was very low. Since the transition from Kindergarten to elementary school is still considered problematic (in 2006, 4.8% of all children of the legal school entrance age delayed school start for 1 year), a new school entry class model has been developed. This new class is not designed so much as a bridge from Kindergarten to elementary school as an introduction to elementary school.

Similar to the situation in the United States, the transition between settings in Germany results in parents being less involved when their children enter formal school.

Japan. In Japan the biggest issue in the transition from nursery school to elementary school is called the "first-grade problem." Children experience a dramatic shift from very child-centered settings, where children have a great deal of autonomy in their activities, to a school setting where cooperation and group identity are highly valued and there is a strong emphasis on academic performance. Significant numbers of children find this transition difficult. Parents want their children to be successful in school, but there isn't really a link between preschool and school. In the 1970s, OECD studied Japanese education and found that there was too much focus on academic success, so the government is reluctant to focus attention on academic goals prior to elementary school. However, parents are focused on academic success, so some send their children to "cram" school before they even start elementary school. In Japan, this transition is seen as a significant issue.

New Zealand. In New Zealand typically developing children are seldom retained in the early years of elementary school. However, a lot of children who have special needs experience a delayed entry to school, staying in early childhood centres until age 6. The relationship between early childhood settings and schools is the weakest component of the strategic plan. Training is offered for teachers of children birth through age 8 as a way to bring people from the different sectors together.

Sweden. In 1998 the preschool class for 6-year-olds was established as a special grade level of school. These classes are part of the elementary school and are seen as helping to accomplish the transition from preschool to school. Compared to preschool for children ages 1 to 5, in the preschool class for 6-year-olds there is more instruction, and the teacher is trained at the same level as other elementary school teachers. Teams of teachers with various competencies support the children's transition from preschool to the preschool class and into the further grades in school. The main difference is that there are goals for children to strive for and attain. Studies in Sweden show that support of the parents is essential for the transition to school.

COMMONALITIES AND CONTRASTS ACROSS THE SIX COUNTRIES

Philosophy, Traditions, and Challenges

Each country has its own set of traditions and philosophical perspectives that have had and continue to have a significant impact on the delivery of services. As these countries face changes in demography, economy, and social change, these philosophies and traditions are often challenged. Many countries in the world, including those included here, owe much to the rich philosophical contributions of Froebel, Pestalozzi, and Montessori. Yet these philosophies have expressed themselves in different ways in the preschool provisions examined here, and they continue to be challenged by today's realities.

France. Longstanding educational traditions provide a strong foundation for both the écoles maternelles and primary schools. In France there is no separate concept of "preschool" culturally. Teachers and parents both think of école maternelle as school even though it is not compulsory. There is a well-established mechanism for alignment between école maternelle and school in the form of teacher collaboration through the cycles, but there is still a significant transition between école maternelle and elementary school. It is a big step forward for children, who are proud to go to elementary school.

Germany. A long history of provision of services to young children marks Germany as a leader in early childhood education. In particular, beginning in the 1800s with Froebel's Kindergarten, Germany has provided a clear model of early childhood education. For centuries both the Protestant and Roman Catholic churches have had a central role in the provision of services right up to the current time. Froebel and other German philosophers have had a profound influence on early childhood education in many nations. This history continues to influence the separation of the early years in kindergarten from the more formal school experience in Germany.

Japan. The Japanese "lesson study" model is well known. Teachers work together to improve their lessons by observing one another, giving feedback, and co-creating an emerging curriculum. This model is used in early childhood education as well. Nursery and kindergarten teachers are very enthusiastic about providing quality education and care, so they use many of the same inquiry methods as teachers in higher levels of school.

In Japanese society the attempt to combine "zest for living" with academic excellence is a source of struggle and is part of the society-wide concern for the balance between making life worthwhile and making a living.

New Zealand. The early childhood curriculum, Te Whāriki, is the guiding force in New Zealand in terms of early education philosophy and tradition. It is made up of four principles and five strands. *Te Whāriki* is the Māori term for "woven mat," which is the metaphor used to promote these interwoven principles and strands. The four principles are *Empowerment, Holistic Development, Family and Community,* and *Relationships.* The five strands are *Well-Being, Belonging, Contribution, Communication,* and *Exploration.* The curriculum is process-oriented rather than content-specific. There is also a separate section written in Māori for Kōhanga Reo and other Māori language-immersion services.

Sweden. There is a strong commitment that schools should be ready for children, and through age 6 the focus can be on social and emotional development. Widespread participation in preschool and the preschool class may be leading in a natural way to earlier school entry. But even up through the elementary grades there is little emphasis on an outcomes-focused approach to school. The work of both Froebel and Robert Owen has been important in establishing a philosophy of early education that emphasizes the integration of care and education. But the philosophy has been influenced by a number of key theorists from Europe and is embedded in a national curriculum in which the state sets the overall values, goals, and guidelines and the local municipalities are responsible for implementation. This current model is consistent across the preschool and school years.

United States. There is no single philosophy guiding early school in the United States. There is no national curriculum for preschool or elementary education. Education and care services for children prior to kindergarten at age 5 developed mainly in response to social and economic changes in United States society and were largely governed by a market-based philosophy—parents paid providers who then responded to what parents wanted at the individual program level. The private sector, including both nonprofit organizations and churches as well as for-profit companies, has played a major role in the expansion of early childhood services prior to school entry. The market-based approach allowed for much variation in the provision of services. While there is a desire for an emphasis on improving children's later academic outcomes through a more direct instructional approach, there is also an emphasis on a child-centered approach with "developmentally appropriate" practices.

Even more than at the preschool level, public schools in the United States have a tradition, going back to the writing of the Constitution, of restricting the influence of the national government on education, with the primary responsibility being at the state level, and a great deal of authority delegated down to the local level for governing schools.

Social and Demographic Factors

France. In France there has been a focus on structures for parents who work, although child care is not always available for working parents who need it in rural areas. Many parents rely on grandparents or a child minder. There is also the issue that working parents are better educated than parents who don't work, and the system should focus equally on the latter's children so that they get the cognitive stimulation that they need.

France is a multicultural society that has chosen not to emphasize the identities of the different ethnic groups, but rather the identity of France as a country and society. The policy toward immigrants is full integration into French society. The most recent curriculum emphasizes this goal. The language of school is French and learning the language is seen as absolutely central to individuals "becoming French" and being full participants in French society. The purpose of education is to transmit the knowledge of humanity, and that knowledge is transmitted through language. Thus a major goal of the early years of education for linguistically diverse children is to master French. Formerly it was thought that it was enough to put the child in an environment that was linguistically rich and the child would acquire the language. Now there is more intentional teaching to provide a solid foundation for language acquisition.

Germany. Like France, Germany has experienced a large influx of immigrants, notably from Turkey and Russia. There is an expectation that 5-year-old children of immigrants will receive a language test and special instruction before they enter school. Little is known about the services being provided or whether children are appropriately assessed, but it is clear that this wave of immigrants presents a challenging set of issues for the early childhood and early school programs in the country. With the union of East and West Germany in the 1990s there was also a major shift in the provision of early childhood services in the eastern portions of the country, with the provisions in the east becoming more like those in western Germany. Also, German students complete their education later than other European students, and there is an interest in lowering this graduation age for the sake of competitiveness. These changes have been at least partially responsible for new questions about when formal schooling should begin in Germany.

Japan. In Japan, the reorganization of the early childhood system has been driven by the declining birth rate, the increase in maternal employment, and the overall restructuring of the welfare state in response to changing demographics. The pressure of the changes has forced a retrenchment of pensions, health, and social services, and the implementation of new measures for financing to expand benefits to more beneficiaries. More attention is being focused on providing care for preschool children while their parents work, and also on supporting stay-at-home mothers. The government has invested heavily in expanding the supply of child care, but there is still a gap between parents' needs and the availability of services. The certified nursery center system used to be operated within the framework of a mandatory placement system, based on the idea that the state has the legal obligation to place a child in a nursery center once the child's need for care is proven. While the government still provides financing, it is no longer responsible for providing child care. Another feature of early childhood services in Japan is that the teacher–child ratios are very high in kindergartens. There are 20 children per teacher for 3-year-olds and 35 per teacher for older children, with no other adults in the room.

It is unclear what the ultimate response to the steep decline in the birth rate and the rapid aging of the population will be. Will the government work to encourage an increase in birth rates, or will its efforts to accommodate the new reality of a different age profile of the population offset the need for such action?

New Zealand. In New Zealand the Ministry of Education governs a lot of different programs with different histories. They came together in part due to the women's movement and the efforts of mothers to create spaces for their children. A second motivating factor was a focus on children's rights. This was a bottom-up process. There is not the demarcation between sectors that is often seen in other countries.

The flexibility offered by the early childhood system has permitted the development of culturally and linguistically appropriate settings for Mäori and Pacific Island children. There are some bilingual classrooms within regular elementary schools, but all children are expected to learn English.

The unifying feature of the New Zealand approach to early education is seen in the national curriculum. Early childhood programs, regardless of their location and parent agency, must follow national Desirable Objectives and Practices in order to be eligible for government funding. While the ministry's 10-year plan is not fully realized yet, New Zealand seems to be settled in its approach toward a system of diverse services at the early childhood level that leads to a common school experience beginning at age 5.

Sweden. Sweden started to build up its preschool sector in the early 1970s to support the family, especially mothers who wanted to work outside the home. This effort was at least partly in response to decreases in the birth rate and concerns about the absolute size of the population. Preschool is now recognized as an important educational experience for children, and in 2001 children of unemployed parents were assured of their right to attend preschool. The move to incorporate all educational services down to the earliest years into the domain of the Ministry of Education has raised the status of preschool and other early childhood services, bringing higher salaries and respect for teachers even though the salaries are not quite at the same level as those of teachers of older children.

Like some of the other countries examined here, Sweden is an increasingly diverse nation due to a large increase in immigration in recent years. It provides strong support to immigrants as they adjust to life there. Early childhood programs strive to provide home language instruction for children, but finding adults who share the children's language can be challenging. Refugee children are diagnosed with psychological and behavior diagnoses at a higher rate than the general population, raising some concerns about the challenges in responding to the increase in diversity in the country.

United States. Demographic changes in the United States have strongly influenced the provision and even the nature of early education. Workforce participation rates and the changing role of women drove the expansion of early care and education provisions, with robust participation by for-profit and nonprofit providers. Increasing urbanization and the resulting concentration of consumers have permitted the array of options in some communities to increase, while rural communities may be underserved. Birth rates in the United States have decreased in parallel with other developed countries; however, immigration rates have offset the declining birth rate—at the same time adding to the diversity of U.S. society. Providing an appropriate education to an increasingly diverse population of students presents challenges to both early childhood and elementary educators, and receives attention from all levels of government.

The increase in the involvement of the public school sector in serving children before kindergarten is a relatively recent phenomenon. A basic question is whether the schools will become the primary providers of education for children beginning at age 4 or even possibly at age 3. If so, this shift will have an increasingly significant impact on the other agencies serving young children. There is already some evidence that the federal Head Start program is shifting to serve somewhat younger children, with a higher proportion of 3-year-olds in the current program and a growing Early Head Start program serving even younger children. About half of the children enrolled in state-funded prekindergarten programs are currently served in private sector settings. It is not clear if this pattern will endure or whether is it a temporary pattern that will evolve into a more fully school-based operation.

In any case, the increasing numbers of 4-year-olds in schools is forcing a rethinking of the early school years. A number of key players, led by private-sector philanthropic foundations and institutions of higher education in the United States, are pushing for a new vision of early schooling, with appropriate educational services for children ages 3 to 8 being seen as the logical organizing frame (see Chapter 1 for further discussion).

As many states in the United States are moving toward universal pre-kindergarten, there is a large and growing interest in thinking of the period from ages 3 to 8 as the first phase of school. Is there a real dichotomy between developmentally appropriate practice and academic learning, or is this an artificial distinction? The authors of this chapter are involved in a major new initiative that is trying to unite the best thinking about early childhood (including developmentally appropriate practice), elementary education, and special education to create what we are calling FirstSchool as the initial educational experience for children in school settings.

CONFRONTING THE FUTURE

In his classic book *Understanding Media*, Marshall McLuhan stated that "the medium is the message" (McLuhan, 1964). He was discussing the widespread availability of television in the middle of the 20th century. His point was that having this new ubiquitous mechanism for the transmission of information available to the masses was a major impact on our society. It was not the content that was so critical, but the very fact that information was now available in a new and more powerful form.

In the same manner, perhaps the most telling feature of early childhood education in the developed countries of the world is simply that it exists. The message to our children is not so much the curriculum of early education as it is the very fact that we offer classroom-based education for children as young as 3, and most children are enrolled. These six countries are shifting toward a heavy reliance on government to support these classrooms in a changing social and economic situation.

Each of these countries has taken major steps toward providing increased and improved education and child care services to families and children. Each has chosen a path that reflects their current reality and at the same time is based on long traditions in their countries. While all of the countries are still making the adjustments, and more change in the education systems even in the short term is a near certainty, there is much we can learn from the ways their systems for educating young children are evolving.

First, there is much agreement across countries in terms of what is important for young children. There is a changed view of children, with an emphasis on children being humans just as much as adults are—with equally valid human rights. In the chapter on New Zealand, Michael Gaffney discusses the introduction of the concept of child rights to the discourse on early education. Children are seen as having a right to a certain number of hours of education, and also a right to the type of setting of the family's choosing. The rights of Mäori and other language-minority children to a culturally and linguistically appropriate setting are strongly defended.

Second, there is some recognition of the need for a balance between the drive for a strong educational intervention and at the same time the need for children to have a good quality of life. The Japanese see this as a life-long struggle to balance "making life worthwhile" and "making a living." In New Zealand children don't go to an early childhood education program only to prepare for school. They go because of needs they have now, to develop their strengths and interests. One expression of these values is seen in the support for programs that preserve a specific cultural heritage while having an overarching national curriculum.

A third commonality among these countries is recognition that the provision of services has a dual function. The evolving status of early childhood education is recognition of the fact that mothers of young children are an indispensable segment of the paid labor force and that this requires new forms of support for services that young families are simply not able to pay for on their own. Concomitantly, there is a vastly expanded view of the learning potential of young children and the impact of early learning on later success in school and life in general. In the United States, there has been financial support for low- and moderate-income families to participate in market-based child care, and a more recent major shift toward involvement of the public school community in providing pre-kindergarten education as an avenue for improving school outcomes for all children. In Sweden a similar shift has occurred. The system was created to support families in having children in an effort to stabilize the birth rate. These services are now under the auspices of the education ministry in recognition of the importance of the early years as the beginning of a life-long learning process.

Fourth, all of the countries are concerned about the transition that children face as they move between early childhood education and care and elementary school. The age of entry to elementary school varies across countries. In New Zealand and the United States, children begin elementary school at age 5, but in the United States there are more and more pre-kindergarten classes in elementary schools for 4- and even 3-year-olds. In France, Germany, and Japan, children begin elementary school at about age 6. However, in Germany children move from Kindergartens operated outside the education system to the formal school, whereas in France children are at écoles maternelles, which are formally linked to elementary schools, from the age of 3 (or even 2 in zones of special priority). In Japan, while kindergartens are considered an educational program, they are quite distinct from elementary schools. And in Sweden, elementary school begins officially at age 7, but the "preschool class" for 6-year-olds is located within school buildings. In most of these countries there are ongoing efforts to understand and improve this transition, without sacrificing essential qualities belonging to either setting. Germany is experimenting with transitional classes and with the new Bildungshaeuser for children aged 3 to 10. The United States has seen a dual interest in children's readiness for school and schools' readiness for children.

In fact, there is a general blurring of school and early childhood education. In the United States, the rapidly expanding pre-kindergarten movement finds about half of the classes in schools and half in the private early childhood sector. In Sweden the move to expand preschool classes in the elementary schools has introduced early childhood pedagogy into schools. In France the move to include children as young as age 2 into the écoles maternelles has put the schools further into the early childhood arena. So perhaps the question is as much "What is school?" as "When do children begin school?"

In this regard, Hans-Guenther Rossbach raised an interesting point of view that challenged our thinking. He said that we construct these different worlds (preschool and school). We say that the transition from preschool to school should be smooth. Is this really the best way? We think in terms of continuity, but maybe discontinuity is not always bad for children. France offers a good example, where the cycle of 3 years includes an experience with some discontinuity that could, in mastering that task, contribute to the development of the child's identity. From the point of view of children we should not refuse them the chance to experience this discontinuity. Children regularly create for themselves challenges about learning, about growing up. Children are proud when they make the move to the "big school." Maybe we should not be as concerned with eliminating the challenges of the transition as with helping children meet the challenges.

At the same time, a fifth commonality is the clear interest in a number of the countries in preserving a distinct early childhood sector. Many countries seem to look at 5- and even 6-year-olds as preschoolers. The government of Japan wants an educational system that helps students to be successful in the world economy, but also wants to promote enjoyment of life and the development of individual talents in a society that is very competitive. In Sweden a conscious effort was made to keep preschool for children ages 1 to 5 separate from school even while bringing these services under the education umbrella. In New Zealand they actively reject the term *preschool*, but use the term *early childhood education*. There is concern in the United States that kindergarten has become too academically focused, and there is active debate between those wanting to include even younger children in the public education system and those who are concerned about protecting young children from inappropriate instructional practices.

Sixth, while all countries are relying more and more on government to pay for early childhood education, countries rely on different levels of government for this support and for policies that establish and govern the programs. In the United States we will almost certainly decide state by state or community by community how we serve children prior to kindergarten. Other countries with more centralized national systems, as opposed to the federal systems of the United States and Germany, have tended to develop their early childhood systems more uniformly, as would be expected. The commitment of France and New Zealand to teacher quality exceeds that of federal systems. In Sweden they use the schools to continually re-create a democratic society. The reality in the United States is that the combination of state governments and a network of local authorities, including local school boards and social service agencies, create a mosaic of services that varies considerably from place to place. A national curriculum might promote unity across the society, but with strong traditions of states' rights, local control, and private enterprise, a strong nonprofit sector, and a society whose diversity is reflected not only in its families but in its early care and education providers, would a national curriculum ever be accepted? The No Child Left Behind Act is sometimes viewed as a back-door national curriculum for kindergarten through high school, and it has been met with strong opposition and resentment. In Japan, kindergarten is education and nursery schools are social services, and efforts to integrate the two systems are instructive for us. Such efforts are difficult even in a situation with a relatively centralized national government. New Zealand has a diverse array of locally based options for families of young children, which now operate within a national structure of funding and standards. New Zealand presents a useful case study for us in how to embrace multiple systems, supporting a diversity of providers but having a unified vision. To point the way forward, they focused on identifying the commonalities. Within the national curriculum, people can see reflected their type of service or their type of center, even though they do things quite differently.

Finally, the demographics of countries have a major influence on policies and practices. Unlike France, Germany, Sweden, and the United States, Japan has not seen a large increase in immigration that to a greater or lesser degree blunts the decline in the birth rate. Japan may well provide a model for how our world can evolve into a place with a stable or even declining total population. The role of early childhood education in this new world is so far not well established, except that its importance to the long-term well-being of society is accepted but its potential is yet to be fulfilled. Just as we have learned from one another about theories of learning, curriculum, and design of programs in the past, we can learn from the policy solutions proposed by other countries as we face common challenges and make choices that will affect children, families, and our society for generations to come.

NOTE

1. The term *Kindergarten* is used in Germany as a generic term for all institutional forms of early childhood care and education for children from age 3 up to the start of compulsory school.

REFERENCES

Clifford, R. M., Cochran, M., & Kagan, S. L. (2003). Challenges for early childhood education and care policy. In D. Cryer & R. M. Clifford (Eds.), *Early childhood education and care in the USA* (pp. 191–210). Baltimore: Paul H. Brookes.

Harms, T., Clifford, R. M., & Cryer, D. (2005). *Early childhood environment rating scale* (rev. ed.). New York: Teachers College Press.

McLuhan, M. (1964). *Understanding media: The extensions of man* (2nd ed.). New York: New American Library.

National Center for Education Statistics. (2004). Computed from National Center for Education Statistics Fast Facts (http://nces.ed.gov/fastfacts/display.asp?id=65) and Brief (NCES 2004-115).

About the Editors
and the Contributors

Richard M. Clifford, Ph.D., is a Senior Scientist at the Frank Porter Graham (FPG) Child Development Institute at the University of North Carolina–Chapel Hill. After serving as a teacher and principal in public schools for more than 25 years, Dr. Clifford has studied public policies and advised local, state, and federal officials and practitioners on policies affecting children and their families. He is currently serving as co-director of the FirstSchool initiative at FPG. He is co-author of a widely used series of instruments for evaluating learning environments for children, and is the author or editor of numerous publications in peer-reviewed journals, books, and reports. He helped establish and served as the first director of the Division of Child Development in the North Carolina Department of Human Resources, and he helped design and implement North Carolina's Smart Start early childhood initiative. He is past president of the National Association for the Education of Young Children.

Gisele M. Crawford, M.A.A., is a Research Specialist at FPG Child Development Institute, University of North Carolina–Chapel Hill. Ms. Crawford has worked on numerous studies of young children and their environments and experiences, including large-scale studies of public pre-kindergartens in the United States. She is currently on the staff of FirstSchool, an initiative to develop a framework for public education for children ages 3 to 8. She has published articles relating to serving diverse populations of children in early childhood programs in the United States.

Diane M. Early, Ph.D., is a Visiting Scholar at FPG Child Development Institute, University of North Carolina–Chapel Hill. Dr. Early is an expert in early childhood care and education in the United States. For 10 years she served as a researcher at FPG Child Development Institute, one of the nation's leading child development research and outreach organizations. In addition to being a Visiting Scholar and consultant with FPG, she is a Research Associate in the Clinical and Social Psychology Department at the University of Rochester. Dr. Early has led several projects investigating classroom quality, teacher preparation and practices, and children's academic and social outcomes in a variety of early care and education settings.

Véronique Francis, Ph.D., is an Assistant Professor at the Institut Universitaire de Formation des Maîtres d'Orléans–Tours, France, and is a member of the *équipe de récherche education familiale et interventions sociales en direction des familles* (research team for family education and social intervention for family welfare) of the Research Centre for Education and Training of the Université Paris X–Nanterre. Her research interests include vulnerable children and their families.

Michael Gaffney, M.A., M.Ed., is the Deputy Director of the Children's Issues Centre at the University of Otago, New Zealand, a national interdisciplinary forum for research into and discussion of children's issues, as well as resources and information for those involved with children. The centre has an educational, research, and policy role, and its main mission is to coordinate, produce, and disseminate information about children's well-being and healthy development. His main areas of study are educational policy in New Zealand, both early childhood education and compulsory schooling, school culture and ethnographic studies, disability studies and inclusive education, and social research methods.

Inge Johansson, Ph.D., is a Professor in the Department of Didactic Science and Early Childhood Education at Stockholm University, Sweden. His research focus is on preschool, early childhood education, and transition.

Stephanie S. Reszka, M.A., is a doctoral student and Research Assistant at the FPG Child Development Institute at the University of North Carolina–Chapel Hill, and is a graduate student in the Early Childhood, Intervention, and Literacy program in UNC's School of Education. Her research interests include early childhood assessment, the quality of early childhood environments, and the social development of children with autism spectrum disorders.

Hans-Guenther Rossbach, Ph.D., is a Professor of Early Childhood Education in the Faculty of Human Sciences and Education at the University of Bamberg, Germany. Dr. Rossbach received his training in education, sociology, and psychology at the Universities of Bonn, Cologne, and Münster. From 1995 to 2002 he was Professor of Education (Didactics/Research of Instruction) at the University of Lueneburg, Germany. Since 2002 he has been at the University of Bamberg. He is the speaker of the research group "Bildungsprozesse, Kompetenzentwicklung und Selektionsentscheidungen im Vor- und Grundschulalter" (Educational Processes, Competence Development and Selection Decisions in Pre- and Primary School Age), sponsored by the German Research Foundation. His research interests include quality in early childhood education, longitudinal research, and evaluation of model programs.

Reiko Uzuhashi, Ph.D., is a Professor of Educational Studies at Shitenoji University, Japan. In 2005, Dr. Uzuhashi was an adjunct fellow at the FPG Child Development Institute at the University of North Carolina–Chapel Hill. She translated the *ECERS-R* and the *ITERS-R* rating scales into Japanese, and her research interests include program improvement and the international comparative study of early childhood education and care through the use of the environment rating scales.

Index